THE JEWS IN GERMANY, 1945–1993

THE JEWS IN GERMANY, 1945–1993

The Building of a Minority

Michael Cohn

 PRAEGER

Westport, Connecticut
London

Library of Congress Cataloging-in-Publication Data

Cohn, Michael.
   The Jews in Germany, 1945–1993 : the building of a minority /
Michael Cohn.
      p.   cm.
   Includes bibliographical references and index.
   ISBN 0–275–94878–1
      1. Jews—Germany—History—1945– 2. Holocaust survivors—
Germany—History. 3. Germany—Ethnic relations.   I. Title.
DS135.G332C64   1994
943′.004924—dc20   94–12045

British Library Cataloguing in Publication Data is available.

Library of Congress Catalog Card Number: 94–12045
ISBN: 0–275–94878–1

First published in 1994

Praeger Publishers, 88 Post Road West, Westport, CT 06881
An imprint of Greenwood Publishing Group, Inc.

Printed in the United States of America

The paper used in this book complies with the
Permanent Paper Standard issued by the National
Information Standards Organization (Z39.48–1984).

10 9 8 7 6 5 4 3 2 1

Dedicated to
Karl A. Wittfogel
and
Dr. Patricia Donovan

Contents

Preface

Germany today is not *Judenfrei*, free of Jews. Approximately 80,000 Jews now live within the borders of the German state. Some are religious Jews, some are not. Some are Jews by the rules of ritual law, some are not. All the Jews in Germany, originally from many countries and believing in many different forms of Judaism, have joined together to create a new minority community that has been given the official title of "Jews in Germany."

This book is an attempt to show how the Jews in Germany have built a social structure that acknowledges the influence of the Holocaust, state Communism and theoretical Socialism, and the establishment of the State of Israel. They have created a new community in Germany built on the ruins of the old.

This process of creating the social structure of a minority should be of interest to more than Jews. Political experts, social historians, and anthropologists must study such developments as the latter half of the twentieth century continues to set ethnic groups adrift from their old homelands. The Muslims of Bosnia, the Hmong of Vietnam, and the Kurds of the Near East either have lost or are in the process of losing their traditional homes. Like the Jews of Germany, they must either build a new identity or disappear.

The problem of identifying precisely who is a Jew is a central issue only to the religiously Orthodox Jews. In this book the definition is more flexible and is based on social rather than religious criteria. We include as Jews all those who identify themselves as such or who are classified as Jews by the members of the majority German population.

The community organization of the Jews in Germany is built on the foundations of the structure of the urban German Jews of pre-1933 Germany. However, events of the last sixty years have caused the Jews of today to change their community from an integrated part of the German society, as the German Jews thought they were then, to a minority community distrustful of the majority with which it interacts. The German majority is also uneasy in its contacts with the Jews in Germany today. The psychological after-effects of World War II continue to influence the thoughts and actions of its survivors, their children and grandchildren, of both Jews and Germans.

The rise of Hitler in 1933, with the enthusiastic consent of most of the citizens of Germany, destroyed the Jewish belief in the permanence of any good will by the Germans toward the Jews. This is true no matter how acculturated the Jews in Germany may seem or what citizenship papers they hold. At the same time, the Holocaust as well as the years of enforced atheism of the Communist governments of Russia, Poland, and East Germany have also changed the culture of the Jews who now live in the newly unified, democratic Germany. With the destruction of the reservoirs of Jewish learning in Eastern Europe, the knowledge of ritual, traditions, and folk culture have been greatly diminished. These reservoirs had not only nourished the self-definition and self-consciousness of Eastern European Jews but that of the German Jews as well. There are many Orthodox Jews today, but a much smaller percentage of Jews who are learned in *Talmudic* lore than there used to be.

The use of the Yiddish language is also much diminished, and Yiddish no longer serves as the *lingua franca* among the various groups of Jews. The culture of the *stedl*, the small Jewish towns and villages of Eastern Europe that constituted the world of Sholom Aleichem and many other writers, no longer influences the culture of the Jews in Germany.

The establishment of the State of Israel has had a massive impact on the Jews in Germany. It has influenced and boosted their self-image, their political consciousness, and their culture. The Israelis now living in Germany have brought their blend of *Ashkenazic*, or European, and *Sephardic*, or Oriental, Jewish traditions with them to replace, in part, the missing world of the ghettos.

The building of a Jewish minority society in Germany is a continuing process; it is not the existence of an encapsulated and static structure. This book is an interim report of that process of building.

No anthropological work can ever be completely neutral—culturally or politically. When dealing with such a sensitive study as the Jews in Germany, it becomes essential therefore to give some information about the background and experiences of the author.

Michael Cohn was born in Leipzig, Germany, in 1924. His maternal grandfather had been active in the Zionist movement prior to his death in 1914. Michael's mother was a group leader in the *Blau-Weiss* (Blue-White), the Zionist youth organization, in Kassel and Leipzig before her marriage in 1920. His father worked in the advertising department of the Jewish community newspaper in Leipzig.

In 1927 the family moved to Berlin where the author's father became active in the German Communist Party. Since he was among those who disagreed with the Communist leadership of 1932 who ordered their members to cooperate with the Nazis in destroying the Social Democrats, he was forced to leave Germany quickly when Hitler assumed power and many of the Communists joined the Nazi Party. His father emigrated to New York in 1933, leaving Michael Cohn and his mother to witness the beginnings of many of the Nazi excesses that would lead to the Holocaust. The author left Berlin in 1934. His family maintained contact with relatives in Germany until they were deported in 1941 and helped many, though by no means all, of his extended family to flee from the German-dominated Europe.

In 1946 the author was sent back to Germany by the U.S. Army. His still-fluent German permitted him to talk freely with both Germans and displaced persons, as refugees were officially known. His work with the German Youth Administration and as editor of an army-camp newspaper allowed him to travel extensively through the U.S. occupation zone. He was a spectator at the trial of the Nazi leadership at Nürnberg and thus had a view of the Nazi Germany, from its arrogant, jack-booted rise to the trial of the husks of its leadership in 1946.

After his discharge from the army in 1947, he returned to Germany in 1951 and in 1971. In 1985 he accepted the invitation of the Berlin Senate to return for a visit to Berlin with his wife, at German government expense. They have returned to Germany every summer form 1990 to 1993 to study the development of the Jewish community in Germany.

Michael Cohn worked as a professional anthropologist at the Brooklyn Children's Museum from 1963 to 1987. The museum is located a few blocks from the world headquarters of the *Lubavitcher Hasidic* movement. He supervised a team of students who studied both that community and the *Satmar Hasidim* in Williamsburg, Brooklyn. During that period he developed a special interest in the study of minorities and border cultures. In addition to his work with Jewish minorities, he also worked with the African American community, helping to plan the excavation of the Free Black community of Weeksville and studying the history of the Black seamen. At present he holds the title of Adjunct Anthropologist, Yeshiva University Museum in New York City. He is a member of the American Anthropological Association and the Society of Professional Archaeologists.

In addition to writing a number of scientific archeological articles he also edited *Jews in Williamsburg* and *Crown Heights and Williamsburg: Two Hasidic Communities* for the Brooklyn Children's Museum and coauthored *Black Men of the Sea* for Dodd, Mead & Co. At the Yeshiva University Museum he was guest curator and author of the catalog for the exhibit *Medieval Justice: The Trial of the Jews of Trent 1475* and was coauthor of the study *From Germany to Washington Heights.*

A preliminary paper of some of the material in this book was given at the American Anthropological Association meeting in San Francisco in December 1992.

ACKNOWLEDGMENTS

Many people helped in the writing of this book. Herbert Harwitt, former member of the *Adass Jisroel* congregation in Berlin and now president of the Mt. Sinai Jewish Center in New York and director of its Holocaust Memorial Library, offered his personal knowledge of Jewish affairs in Germany and the use of the library resources at the Center. Sylvia Herskowitz, Director of the Yeshiva University Museum, has given me constant encouragement. Dr. Klaus Herrmann of Concordia University, Montreal, Canada, kept feeding me both data and sources of additional information. Dr. John Strauss of Yale University guided me to sources of psychological research.

In Germany I had the total cooperation of the Berlin Jewish *Gemeinde*, the use of its excellent library and the help of its late chairman, Heinz Galinski, and its present head, Jerzy Kanal. Dr. Irene Runge of the *Jüdischer Kulturverein* made herself and her writings always available. Dr. Hermann Simon and Dr. Peter Kirschner told me much about the Jews in East Germany. The *Gemeinden* of Hamburg and Munich offered both their hospitality and information. Many others in Germany, both Jews and Germans, were willing to answer difficult questions.

Sol Kagan, executive director of the Conference on Jewish Material Claims Against Germany, and Rabbi Herschel Gluck, of the *Chabad Lubavitch* in London, were always prompt and courteous in answering inquiries. Rabbi Gluck allowed us time from his busy schedule to be interviewed in London. Special mention must also be made of the help given by the German consulate, the Goethe Haus, and the German Information Service in New York.

Living in New York City allows easy access to the magnificent collections of books and documents housed at the Leo Baeck Institute, the Judaic division of the New York Public Library, and at the YIVO Institute for Jewish Research. To them and to the many other helpers who have not been specifically mentioned much thanks is due.

My wife, Susan Strauss Cohn, has worked with me on many phases of this book. She shared in my research, edited my English, and argued about some of my conclusions from her viewpoint as a third-generation American Jew. Without her help and patience this would have been a lesser book or would not have come into existence at all.

Michael Cohn

Chapter One

The Community of the Jews in Germany[1]

The Jewish Community, a social as well as a religious body, is the core of the conception of the Jewish minority in Germany. At present some 36,000 to 40,000 Jews are dues-paying members of these legally and geographically defined units.[2] The *Gemeinde*, or *Kahilla* in Hebrew, is more than a congregation.[3] There may be more than one congregation or synagogue in a given city or town, but there is only one *Gemeinde*.[4] This is a corporate body of Jews recognized by the German government and regulated as a quasi-governmental agency. All the various German constitutions since 1848, except at a time near the end of the Nazi era, allow complete freedom of choice of religion to all citizens or allow them to practice no religion at all. However, there is not the total separation of church and state in Germany as is found in the United States under its constitution. Even the Communist government of the now-defunct German Democratic Republic (DDR) had a department for religious affairs. This government department had recognized the existence of Jewish *Gemeinden* in eight cities in 1989. However, the total registered membership of these recognized communities numbered only 1200 Jews altogether, most of them elderly.[5] There were many more unregistered Jews than there were officially registered community members living in East Germany in 1989, but membership in a religious body was detrimental to anyone seeking social or economic advancement. Communism was definitely antireligious, hostile to all of them as far as that was politically possible. The number of Jews living in the other half of Germany in 1989, the *Bundesrepublic* (West Germany), both registered as community members and unregistered, was much larger. Berlin has about 9,500 members in its *Gemeinde*, Frankfurt 7500, Munich 5000, and Hamburg 2500. Christian religious bodies, both Catholic and Protestant, are recognized the same way as the Jewish *Gemeinde* by the government, although their memberships number in the millions each. This pattern of governmental recognition and support was true of the German imperial government of 1871–1918, the Weimar Republic of 1919–1933, the Bundesrepublic 1948–1990, and the unified German government of today. Even the Nazi government recognized the Jewish *Gemeinden* as legal bodies until June 10, 1943.[6] Membership rolls and lists of officers are registered with the government, and the government collects the membership dues as part of the income tax. The appropriate total collected is then forwarded to the *Gemeinde* treasury. At present, the religious membership fee is about eight percent on top of the income tax payment.

There are some congregations of Jews in the United States that are also organized on the basis of a total *Gemeinde*, or *Kahilla*. These religious groups have their own synagogues, ritual baths, schools, social services, and even stores recognized as ritually pure by their own rabbis. However, these groups in the United States only cover a narrow segment rather than the broad band of Jewish thought covered by a German *Gemeinde*. The *Hasidic* communities in Orange County, N.Y., and the neo-Orthodox *Jeshurun* congregation in the northern part of Manhattan come to mind. These communities in the United States are not government-supported, although they may obtain government money for specific social services. They must open those services, however, to use by all residents of the locality, a condition often not acceptable to the very Orthodox. The German *Gemeinde* need not open any of its services to anyone except its members, and it can also set the standards for membership in the community.

The right of the German *Gemeinde* to represent all the Jews of a community and to determine who is a Jew was challenged with the passage of the *Austrittsgesetz*, the law governing Jews who wished to leave the *Gemeinde* without losing their status as Jews. This law was enacted by the Prussian Parliament in 1876. Anyone who wished to leave the community had to file a formal notice with the town clerk, since membership had a bearing on the amount of taxes to be collected. The *Austrittsgesetz* was an acknowledgment that the institution of the old ghettos was truly dissolved and that every Jew was now free to define his or her form of Jewishness.

This law also allowed dissident Jews to set up their own *Gemeinde* and to apply to the government for recognition as a separate religious organization. Relatively few of these dissident bodies were ever recognized by the government as *Gemeinden*, since the authorities much preferred to deal with a single Jewish entity rather than a multiplicity of quarreling congregations. Religious groups that did not receive official recognition as *Gemeinde* were and are treated as if they were private clubs or charitable organizations. This system applies to the many dissident sects of all religions, not just to Jews. Of course it is perfectly possible for a group of Jews to set up their own congregation or *Talmud* study circle without leaving the *Gemeinde*. The individual members, however, must still meet the membership standards of the *Gemeinde*. This ability to remain as members of the community is also true of Jews who choose not to worship at the synagogue at all. As long as they are of Jewish birth and raise their children as Jews they would not be expelled. The flexibility allows the community to encompass a wider variety of opinions and retain its members even in cases of minor disagreements on ritual or policy.

The advantages to the individual who chooses to retain his affiliation without attending services is that the *Gemeinde* offers so much more than just religious services. It is the *Gemeinde* that controls or at least supervises a large group of social services. It sets up day care, summer camps, schools, hospitals, old-age homes, and cemeteries. It controls various forms of social welfare payments and licenses kosher establishments. Through the Conference of Jewish Material Claims Against Germany, it has access to money due as reparations for damages done under the Nazis. Jewish communities reestablishing themselves in places where there has been no Jewish community for fifty years can apply for the return of real estate formerly owned by the Jewish community in the 1930s. This may allow the rebuilt *Gemeinde* to start out with a building and a cemetery of its own and possibly with funds derived from property that had been destroyed by the Nazis or through the war. This has been happening, especially in East Germany, where the whole process of reparations payments is still in its initial stages.

The *Zentralrat* (Central Council of the Jews in Germany) and especially its chairman coordinate the work of all the local *Gemeinden* in Germany and deal with the German government on behalf of all the Jews in Germany. The *Zentralrat* publishes a weekly newspaper, the *Allgemeine Jüdische Wochenzeitung* (the General Jewish Weekly Newspaper). This paper publishes all the announcements of interest to the Jewish community, services in synagogues all over Germany, commercial and personal announcements, as well as obituaries. Non-Jewish politicians and business firms use this paper to reach Jewish constituents. There are a number of other newspapers and bulletins published by the various local communities, but the *Allgemeine* is expected to reach all the Jews in Germany, even those in dissident groups. It is sometimes sold at newsstands and bookshops in addition to being available at all Jewish community centers.

Election to a governing body of a *Gemeinde* can be a full-scale political campaign fought out by individuals or lists of candidates representing philosophical, religious, or political differences. Since most cities have only one *Gemeinde* the Jewish leadership tries to include a range of viewpoints on the list of candidates and so avoid bitter internal battles. As in all politics, there are times when such tactics do not work. However, even when an election has been bitterly fought, as was the case recently in Berlin, compromises can be arranged after the election. In the Berlin election the "Liberal-Jewish" list, representing the present leadership, captured eleven seats on the governing council; its opposition "Democratic List," representing an alliance of various dissidents, took ten. There was a formal motion in the council after the election that no member of the council would be identified in the newsletter by his or her "party."

Ignatz Bubis, the present head of the *Zentralrat*, wrote a letter to the *Allgemeine* on his inauguration that his aim was the creation of "Unity Communities" (*Einheitsgemeinden*) in which Liberal, Conservative, and Orthodox would find themselves comfortable or at least would find no insurmountable barriers to their belonging.[7] In large cities like Berlin, this all-inclusiveness is made easier for the *Gemeinde* by the fact that there are a number of synagogues whose worshippers differ in details of ethnic origin or in ritual without disrupting the fabric of the *Gemeinde*.

It is important to explain what the *Gemeinde* is not. Because of its size and somewhat bureaucratic organization, the *Gemeinde* cannot by itself form the basis for the tight social bonds of friendship and social intercourse needed in a truly cohesive community. It is simply too big and clumsy to function as a club. If tight bonds are formed within the *Gemeinde*, they are usually based on smaller groupings such as members of a school class, a joint activity such as raising money for a specific charity, or a social activity. An increasing number of such groupings range from the parents of children in the day-care center to membership in WIZO, the Women's Zionist Organization.

There are also deep social divisions within the community, often based on ethnic origin. As one Jew of Polish origin told us, "We play rummy and poker, the German Jews sit at home and play bridge." The German Jews have always separated themselves from the Eastern Jews, and the Jews of Polish origin separate themselves in turn from the Russian immigrants. Such ethnic divisions can be overemphasized since all the Jews recognize that they share their Jewishness, but the cleavages exist nonetheless. Israelis also form a separate grouping, and the newly arrived Americans also tend to cluster. These groupings are not only social, but they are also likely to lead to the formation of networks of economic cooperation.

The full spectrum of groupings as they existed in the prewar *Ashkenazic Kahilla* have not yet been reestablished in the Jewish communities in Germany today, and some of them are actually unnecessary today. The groups that provided poor girls with dowries or that washed and dressed the bodies of the deceased members are anachronisms. The small groupings that studied and discussed the *Talmud*, the Hebrew oral traditions written down after the destruction of the Temple in 71 A.D. and studied and commented on by scholars since then, have also largely disappeared in Germany.[8]

One of the functions of the community that has grown much larger and more important today is the care of Jews from other communities. In today's terms that means helping the refugees from Russia and from the other former republics of the Soviet Union as well as the refugees from the civil wars in what had been Yugoslavia. The basic needs of these refugees may be met by the German social network, but their many special needs become the burden on the Jews in Germany. Until they can stand on their own feet, these refugees need advice on dealing with the German bureaucracy; social, medical, and psychological specialists; and help in establishing social groups. As the German immigration policy tightens, there will also be refugees who have slipped into the country illegally and who are not covered by the social network. That is an old problem which is again becoming acute.

There are a large number of Jews who are members of the *Gemeinde* but who go to the synagogue only on the High Holy Days or not at all. Some may be agnostics but others may be very Orthodox. A Jewish synagogue is, after all, only a meeting house, not a temple. Ten male Jews age thirteen or older are enough to hold services. They constitute a *Minya* (a congregation) by Jewish ritual law. No rabbi or priest is needed to hold formal prayer services, which can also be led by a knowledgeable elder. Many of the prayer services, such as the lighting of the Sabbath candles, the Passover services, and the building of the *Succoth* (an outdoor hut for the harvest festival in fall) are celebrated in the home.

It is the *Gemeinde*, not the synagogue, that controls much of the Jewish life. Therefore, the role of the rabbi is often smaller than that of the chairman of the *Gemeinde*. It is the chairman or a committee appointed by him that hires the rabbi and very often supervises the hiring of the rest of the staff as well. The rabbi, in turn, controls the form of the services and the ritual. He is also a teacher and a personal counselor to members of the congregation. He performs marriages, conversion to the Jewish faith, and similar activities in accordance with his interpretation of Jewish law. In some countries, decisions on these matters can be appealed to a *Beth Din* (a Jewish court) but such institutions are only rudimentary in Germany because of the shortage of rabbis. Members who disagree with the rabbi simply leave the congregation and often the *Gemeinde* as well. Disputes between the rabbi and the chairman of a congregation or the *Gemeinde* are not unknown, but is almost invariably the rabbi who resigns his post in these disputes.

Forms of ritual in most of the synagogues in Germany that are members of the *Gemeinden* range from Liberal to the Orthodox. Differences in their form of worship may include whether or not an organ and a choir are used, whether men and women are seated together or separately, and similar details. A special problem for the Orthodox who live in cities without their own synagogue is that they often live beyond walking distance of the synagogue, thus forcing them either to travel on the Sabbath or to stay over at someone's home. Most of the prayer books in use today are reprints of the German Jewish prayer books first published prior to 1933. They represent an acceptable common denominator at present. There are few disputes today on ritual matters, unlike in the past.

Very few of the Jews in Germany today—whether of German, Israeli, or Russian origin—are skilled in debating questions of Jewish ritual law, a subject that formed a major part of the religious interest prior to 1933. Social and economic concerns rank higher among the Jewish population of the present than do questions of ritual. It is likely that this order of importance will remain the same even when the post-Holocaust generation comes to power.

The chairman of the *Zentralrat* is considered the spokesman for all the Jews in Germany, despite the fact that probably half the Jews in Germany are not members of the *Gemeinde* or did not vote and so had no voice in choosing him. If the government or the press needs a public statement or needs a Jew on a public platform, it is usually the chairman of the *Zentralrat* or the chairman of the local *Gemeinde* rather than a rabbi who performs that function. It is the chairman of the *Zentralrat* who controls the appointments of representatives of the Jews in Germany to national or international bodies such as the World Jewish Congress or the Conference of Jewish Material Claims Against Germany. The chairman of the *Zentralrat* or the *Gemeinderat* oversees the allocation of *Gemeinde* funds. That social agencies who represent his viewpoints do better than those who do not is a normal development under such a system.

The chairmen are not rabbis and do not need to be especially skilled in *Talmudic* law. Mr. Bubis, the present head of the *Zentralrat*, fled from Breslau, Silesia (now Wroclaw, Poland), to Deblin, Poland. Four years later the German army marched in and Mr. Bubis found himself in a Nazi labor camp. After the war he became a dealer in precious metals and eventually settled in Frankfurt, where he entered the real-estate market and became a very wealthy businessman. It is his business acumen and his having survived the Holocaust that made him first the head of the Frankfurt community and later head of all the Jews in Germany. Piety was not an issue, and his personal background certainly had given him little time for religious studies.

His predecessor, Heinz Galinski, was also a survivor of the concentration camps, not a *Yeshiva* (religious school). He was an administrator and a politically skilled infighter, not a scholar, when he was selected to head the Berlin *Gemeinde* in 1949. In the years after the war, it was Heinz Galinski, the politician, who led the fight for the recognition of the Jews in Germany as a community in their own right instead of as a group of Jews waiting to emigrate elsewhere. It was he who dealt politically with the various West German administrations. When we interviewed him in 1990, he typically dismissed the various Jewish dissidents outside the *Gemeinde* as political rather than ritually oriented nuisances.[9]

Chairmen of the *Gemeinde* can be women as well as men. The Munich *Gemeinde* has been led for years by Charlotte Knobloch, a descendant of an old, established Munich Jewish family. However, women chairpersons represent a problem for Orthodox congregations, especially those without full-time rabbis. Among the Orthodox, women are not considered suitable to handle ritual matters and, under certain conditions, are limited in their contacts with men.

The *Gemeinden* of various cities play a special role beyond their borders. Frankfurt is probably not only the wealthiest, but also the most stable and in many ways the most conservative of the Jewish communities in Germany. Its newspaper, the *Frankfurter Nachrichten*, rivals the *Allgemeine* in size. The Frankfurt community is based in part on the *Landjuden*, the Orthodox village Jews who have lived in Germany for centuries. Its membership is second only to the Berlin community in size and it has fewer Russian refugees than does Berlin. Frankfurt is traditionally associated with the Rothschilds, and their banking house still maintains a branch there and advertises in the Jewish paper.

Munich's Jewish community is known for its active art program and its work with Jewish youth. This year it issued the avant guard *Jews Week* dealing with Lenny Kravitz and rock music as well as other subjects of interest to youth. Its art shows have travelled to other towns for exhibition, and it has employed a *Lubavitcher Hasidic* rabbi to supplement its staff.

Berlin is by far the largest Jewish community in Germany, with nearly 10,000 members. It is also the only city where there are significant organized groups of dissident Jews. Membership in the community has been rising at a rate of more than ten percent a year for the last three years. It is the most politically active community and will probably increase as the capital of Germany shifts gradually from Bonn to Berlin. At the moment the *Allgemeine* is still published in Bonn, although it maintains an office in Berlin. The central office for Jewish social services is in Frankfurt and will likely remain there. Two large Jewish bookstores have recently been established and serve as centers for public readings and concerts. One is in Munich and the other is in Berlin. Other bookstores are also beginning to handle books about the Jewish community and the Holocaust.

The *Allgemeine* lists forty-one Jewish communities in West Germany and eight in the "new" states, the former East Germany. Some of these have only 150–200 members and even then may represent a region rather than an individual town. This is true in West Germany as well as in the East. The future development of these widespread, small Jewish communities will continue to be an interesting study for the future.

The origins of the modern *Gemeinde* can be traced back to the ghettos as they existed both in the cities and the rural districts of Germany in the eighteenth century.[10] Though there are records of Jews in Germany since Roman times, it was the Thirty Years' War (1618–1648) that allowed many Jews to drift into Germany from the Austrian Empire. Jewish settlement was especially noticeable in the areas along the Rhine and in Silesia. These areas had been especially devastated during the war, and their population was greatly diminished by the long and bitter fighting. That war had begun as a religious controversy between Protestants and Catholics, and at its end, religious orthodoxy of all kinds stood at a discount. Rulers were glad to attract anyone who could and would pay taxes and replace the war dead.

When we examine the laws of the seventeenth and eighteenth centuries that governed the life of the Jews of that time, we find that the Jews were mostly dealt with in terms of whole communities, corporate bodies rather than individuals. The body of Jews might be the residents in a particular town or the total Jewish population of a region or principality. Thus, in law, all the Jews of Bavaria or Prussia were dealt with as a unit.[11] It is upon that unit that taxes or forced contributions were imposed, and it was the total community that was given certain rights of self-government.[12] The Jewish community as a corporate body took care of the sick, handled welfare, education, ritual matters, and the care of visiting Jews from other Jewish communities. Sometimes Jewish communities were also given the right to impose fees on Jews from outside the community who wished to trade in the local market. Some Jews, usually wealthy or well connected, received a document directly from the ruler giving them the power to settle in a town or region. They were thus somewhat independent from the Jewish authorities of the ghetto. These wealthy Jews were the *Schutzjuden* (protected Jews). Naturally, such a privileged status demanded a special contribution to the ruler by the Jewish recipient of the privilege. If the protection was to extend to the entire family of the *Schutzjude*, that meant another contribution. Some Jews even received the right to appear at court, *Hofjuden*. Some of the *Hofjuden* served the ruler directly as finance minister or mint master. Neither of these jobs made the Jews very popular among the general Christian population. Joseph ben Issacher Susskind Offenbach, the *Jud Süss* of the famous Lionel Feuchtwanger novel by that name, served as finance minister to the state of Würtemberg, 1732–1738. At the death of his patron, Offenbach was accused of embezzlement and was hanged.[13] The brothers Veitel, Daniel, and Ephraim Itzig became mint masters for Frederick the Great in 1760. The profits from that appointment allowed Ephraim to build a fine house only two years later. The house is still standing in Berlin today and serves as a museum. The Prussian population was less than enthusiastic about the debasement of the Prussian coinage ordered by Frederick but

carried out by Ephraim Itzig. "*Aussen schön, innen schlimm.
Aussen Friederich, innen Ephraim*" (Outside lovely, inside bad.
Outside Frederick, inside Ephraim), ran the popular verse concern-
ing these silver-coated copper thalers. "Itzig" remained a derogatory term for Jews among Berliners for more than 200 years.

The role of the protected and court Jews was more than just
economic. Moses Mendelsohn (1729–1786) was both a factory
owner and a philosopher. He corresponded with many of the leading
intellectuals of the Enlightenment in Europe. Among other writings, he translated the first five books of the Bible into German and
provided that translation with a Hebrew commentary. This volume
served many Jews as their first introduction to German. Mendelsohn also was the model for the title figure in the well-known play
Nathan the Wise by the German dramatist Lessing. In 1778 Isaac
Daniel Itzig and David Friedlander founded the Jewish Free School
in Berlin, where classes were taught in both Hebrew and German,
a system followed today by most Jewish schools.

The Jews of the Enlightenment found themselves under attack
from two sides. The Orthodox rabbis attacked them for daring to
"water down" the traditional Judaism as it was at that time. At the
same time, the "enlightened" Jews were under considerable pressure from the society around them to convert to Christianity. Two
of Mendelsohn's daughters followed this path to a pro forma
conversion, as did the poet Heinrich Heine. Although they gained
formal civil rights by baptism, these converts soon found that the
Jews considered them Christians as well as traitors to their Jewish
heritage, and the Christians generally considered them still to be
Jews. This fate not only met Heine but also the composer Felix
Mendelssohn. Even today, conversion from Judaism leaves converts in this ambivalent position, not just in Germany, as the British
prime minister Disraeli found out.

Most crafts, professions, and trade as well as ownership of land
outside the ghettos was barred to Jews until the middle of the
nineteenth century. As a result, peddling and trading became a
Jewish activity. In many of the villages along the Rhine and in

Würtemberg, Jews engaged in horse- and cattle-trading and pur-chased wheat from the peasants. From there it was only a short step for the Jews to become butchers and bakers. At the same time the Jews also made small loans to the villagers who were in need of ready cash, loans secured on chattels or cattle. In Silesia, Jews also bought up the home-loomed linens from the villages. If these Silesian peddlers flourished, they found themselves with the nec-essary capital to take advantage of the Industrial Revolution and set up linen factories and wholesale establishments. Thus, much of the textile trade with its international connections came into Jewish hands. Some of the Jewish families, such as the Rothschilds, became wealthy enough to establish private banks. Some of these banks, like those of the Warburgs of Hamburg, survive today.

All of these activities left the Jews in Germany with a reputation for being financially shrewd, wealthy, and unscrupulous in their dealings. This historically based image of Jews as money lenders and exploiters of German peasants still persists and is often attrib-uted erroneously to all Jews.

On the other hand, the ability of the Jewish community to raise cash or to make a sizeable contribution to a government in exchange for laws favoring Jews or rescinding restrictions affecting all Jews is also traditional. We will say more about the relationships between Jews and Germans in later chapters.

The Jews in Germany also maintained a tradition of learned rabbis. These teachers were not known for their official position or their wealth but for their great learning. Their opinions circulated widely in the Jewish communities, spread by word of mouth or by pamphlets and books. For example, Rabbi Jacob Emden Ashkenazi (1698–1776) held no official position in any congregation for most of his life. Yet his prestige was great enough that he was able to engage the official rabbi of the communities of Hamburg and Altona, Rabbi Jonathan Eybeschutz (1690–1764), in what has since become known as the "Great Debate." The subject matter of that dispute may no longer be important to us, but the fact that such an ideological dispute could disrupt the entire Jewish community is worth noting. Though the dispute was carried on primarily by sermon and pamphlet, it became sufficiently violent to cause a near-riot on the Hamburg Stock Exchange.[14]

The emancipation of the Jews and the breakup of the ghettos (1812–1869), when Jews were given their full civil rights, did not end this tradition of Jewish scholarship. In the 1930s such scholars included Martin Buber (b. 1878), translator and philosopher; Isaac Breuer (b. 1878), leader of the neo-Orthodox separatist movement; and Leo Baeck (b. 1873), leader of Progressive Judaism. Noticeably, all of these scholars were already elderly when Hitler came to power, so when death or exile removed them from the scene, there were no successors. The Holocaust prevented the development of new Jewish philosophers. Such Jewish leaders as developed in Germany and Eastern Europe in the 1930s had to be more concerned with their own physical survival and that of their communities than with scholarly debate. After the war the practical rather than philosophical problems connected with the survivors of the extermination camps and the establishment of the State of Israel absorbed the attention of world Jewry to the diminution of traditional scholarship. Since World War II no new scholarly figure has arisen in Germany to challenge the status of the politically oriented chairmen of the *Zentralrat*. The absence of any formal, religious training facility such as a rabbinical *yeshiva* in Germany and the absence of the traditional study groups that formerly studied and debated *mishnah* (oral law) ensure that rabbis in Germany will be imports from Israel or the United States for the foreseeable future. Serious religious controversies such as the sale of land of the old Hamburg cemetery (see Chapter Two) are referred to the rabbis in Israel for arbitration. On the other hand, the Jews in Germany are reassuming a serious economic role in Germany, a subject that will be discussed further in later chapters.

This emphasis today on the social and cultural aspects of the ritual side of Judaism can be sensed when one looks at the physical plant of the Jewish communities in some of the major German cities. The Berlin Jewish community center on the *Fasanenstrasse* was built on the site of an old synagogue that was destroyed during the *Kristallnacht* in 1938. The rebuilt center, dedicated in 1959, contains the offices of the *Gemeinde*, meeting rooms, a library, and a kosher restaurant but no synagogue; the meeting rooms can and have been used for services on occasion.[15] The five functioning synagogues that are members of the *Gemeinde* are located elsewhere. Elsewhere also are the Jewish schools, the day-care center and old-age home, and facilities for other functions. The "New Synagogue" (built 1876) is the "Centrum Judaicum," which will be discussed elsewhere. The same pattern is true in Frankfurt, where both Jews and non-Jews are attracted by lectures and art exhibits at the community centers, not the synagogue. In Hamburg the offices that deal with the daily business of the *Gemeinde* are located more than a kilometer from the synagogue and community center, which is kept locked except when services or activities are being held. Only in Munich is there a joint address for the synagogue and the *Gemeinde* offices. Whether this pattern of separating administration, cultural affairs, and ritual activities will persist remains to be seen.

In Berlin a central area of Jewish activity is developing around the "New Synagogue," even though there is no building that now functions as a synagogue. Nearby are the offices that formerly housed the East Berlin *Gemeinde*, which is now used for social services. Nearby also is the new Jewish high school, also used for public lectures, an art gallery for Jewish artists, and the two Jewish restaurants: one strictly kosher maintained by the dissident *Adass* congregation (see Chapter Two); the other featuring Israeli food. The two dissident groups, the *Adass* and the *Jüdischer Kulturverein*, meet nearby, and the old *Ryckastrasse* synagogue with its old cemetery is within walking distance.

This is the area of the old *Scheunenviertel* (cattle barn district) primarily inhabited by Jews of Russian and Polish origin prior to 1933, which was known then for its illegal peddlers and prostitutes as well as for its Orthodox Jews. It was separated both physically and psychologically from the district near the *Fasanenstrasse* and the *Kurfürstendamm* inhabited by the Westernized German Jews. Today the *Scheunenviertel* again has its "not quite respectable" activities, discos and "hippy" cafes. It will be interesting to see whether the old ethnic divisions will repeat themselves together with the political differentiation between left-wingers and the main-stream parties that is now quite noticeable.

These ethnic, cultural, and political differences within the Jewish community do not occur only in Berlin; they are also present or incipient in other communities in Germany. They add to rather than detract from the Jewish presence, and officially at least, there is no attempt to destroy this diversity. We will come back to the subject of Jewish acculturation in Chapter Three.

The inclusive social and cultural activities sponsored by the *Gemeinde* have an effect on the life of almost all Jews in Germany. Even nonreligious Jews are likely to want to send their children to Jewish day-care centers and summer camps. Such institutions are an economic necessity for families where both parents work outside the home or for single-parent families. Such institutions are even more a cultural imperative for Jews in Germany. These facilities provide an opportunity for Jewish enculturalization for Jewish children. Because of the Holocaust as well as Lenin's and Stalin's antireligious and anti-Hebraic policies, many parents have lost contact with Jewish traditions. Children can learn about such traditions in the day-care centers, summer camps, and group activities. There they can sing Hebrew songs, celebrate the holidays, enjoy Jewish cooking, and make Jewish friends. If the *Gemeinde* cannot find adequate teachers at home to teach these things, they have the means and connections to import the teachers from Israel and the United States. In these institutions, too, the new form of Jewishness is being built by the *Gemeinde* rather than by the individual rabbis. It will be an urban German Jewish tradition rather than the tradition of Eastern Europe. There will also be strong Israeli overtones, since almost all of the teachers, wherever they were born, are trained in Israel. A few students from Germany are being sent to study in

Orthodox schools both in England and in Israel, but that is a very expensive option, possible only for the very wealthy.

Child care is one way the *Gemeinde* uses to recruit and retain members. Concerts, lectures, and other cultural events are also used to attract Jews and strengthen group cohesion. Another important tool to promote group cohesion is the fact that the *Gemeinde* controls the Jewish cemeteries. In almost all Jewish families there is at least one member who places value on tradition. This makes cremation, illegal by Jewish ritual law, unpopular. A proper Jewish burial and a place to say prayers for the dead gives everyone a sense of cohesion and continuity. In the communities that are now being reconstituted, particularly those in the former East Germany, the presence of the old Jewish cemeteries helps the new members feel that they are a continuation, not a pioneering community. Very few of the Orthodox Jews have the means and the will to have their bodies shipped to Israel for burial in sacred soil. The ritual rules that require burial within twenty-four hours of death make burial in Israel a rare occurrence, even for those who have not felt "at home" in Germany. The emotion that cemeteries are so important in giving a sense of continuity makes the desecration of gravestones and cemeteries by Neo-Nazis such a psychologically shocking event. The existence of the old graves of the families of German Jewish emigrants is also a powerful factor in bringing them back for at least a visit to their old hometowns, alone or with their children.

The reverse side of this Jewish social cohesion is the maintenance of barriers to social intercourse between Jew and German. Only if both sides have strong joint objectives such as in politics, in business, or in the universities can this social division be overcome.

Special mention must be made of the problem faced by members and offspring of mixed marriages between Jew and non-Jew. These marriages exist not only between Jews and Germans, but also between Jews and the many other nationalities resident in Germany. By *halachic* or Jewish ritual law, Jewish descent is determined by the religion of the mother. By that law the child of a Jewish father and non-Jewish mother is not a Jew. The *Gemeinde* follows that definition for membership of the Jewish community in order to retain Orthodox and Conservative members. Yet modern life brings Jew and non-Jew into contact. Even some students of the new Jewish high school are Christians. Relationships and marriages happen despite the rebukes and head-shakings of the elders.

In addition, the special provisions the Nazis made for Jews married to non-Jews, half-Jews, and quarter-Jews in the language of the time makes it more likely that members of such marriages avoided deportation to the death camps. They and their children represent a considerable portion of the Holocaust survivors in Germany. We will examine the problems of these people, who are not quite accepted as members of any religious group, again and again in the discussions in this book. It is a problem that concerns Jews all over the world, not just Jews in Germany.

Jews from Russia often face problems in proving their Jewish identity under ritual law. This may be due to a mixed marriage, lack of male circumcision, or an inability to prove Jewish matrilineal descent. They usually feel themselves to be Jews and are considered Jews by both the German and Russian population even though they may not be recognized as Jews by the *Gemeinde*. They could, of course, go through the difficult steps of Jewish conversion, but that would mean having to admit that they had not been Jews in the first place. Most of them drift into a secular Jewish existence. They may not even list themselves as Jews in the German census, a process that creates a considerable undercount of the number of Jews in Germany.

We can see how the *Gemeinde* binds most of the Jewish community together and, by that very activity, isolates them socially from their German neighbors. The *Gemeinde* and its spokesmen are considered representatives of all Jews in Germany, whether members or not. It is the *Gemeinde* that tries to define the term "Jew," and it is that definition and the norms of the *Gemeinde* that constitute the scale on which all Jews in Germany must be measured.

Since there are the norms of the *Gemeinde*, we can define the Jews in Germany as an ethnic as well as a religious minority with its own political and social structure. There are deviants within this minority, but they often share more with the minority than with the majority. This Jewish minority is living in Germany, and its members may be German citizens. But citizens or not, Jews are clearly set apart from the general group defined as Germans. The increasing number of Jews in Germany and the increasing number of Jewish communities may increase the size of this minority, but they do not challenge its status as an ethnic minority called the "Jews in Germany." It is a minority that not only differs from the German majority; it also differs from the other minorities living in Germany and from the Jews living in other countries culturally.

NOTES

1. The term "Jews in Germany" includes all Jews living within the physical borders of today's Germany. The term "German Jews" describes those Jews who share the culture of the German Jews as it existed prior to 1933 and who also hold German citizenship.

2. The number of Jews living in Germany is a subject of much speculation and dispute. The number of 36,000 to 40,000 includes only members of the Jewish *Gemeinden*, not the total number of Jews in Germany.

3. See a general discussion in Gertrude Hirschler, ed., *Ashkenaz, The German Jewish Heritage* (New York: Yeshiva University Museum, 1988).

4. For exceptions to this rule, see Chapter Two.

5. *Nachrichten Blatt des Verbandes der Jüdischen Gemeinden in der DDR* (Berlin: DDR, March 1989).

6. Bilderarchiv Preussichen Kulturbesitz, *Juden in Preussen* (Dontmund: Harenberg Kommunikation, 1981) p. 397.

7. *Allgemeine Judische Wochenzeitung* (Bonn, 24 Sept. 1992).

8. For discussion of these groups, see Hirschler, ed., *Ashkenaz.*

9. Interview, Berlin, June 1990.

10. Hirschler, *Ashkenaz*, pp. 57–101.

11. Isador Silbernagl, ed., *Verfassung und Verwaltung Samtlicher Religionsgemeinschaften in Bayern* (Regensburg, 1900).

12. Eric Zimmer, *The Kahillah: The Communal Life and Organization of Ashkenazic Jewry* in *Ashkenaz*.

13. Judging by the large number of engravings of this event known, the death of "Jew Süss" must have been very popular. For an example of such engraving, see *Ashkenaz*, p. 272.

14. Ibid., p. 67.

15. H. G. Selethin, *Geschichte der Juden in Berlin*, Festschrift der Jüdischen Gemeinde (Berlin: 1959).

Chapter Two

Alternative Jewish Groupings

There are a number of alternative Jewish groupings that represent a wide variety of viewpoints available to those Jews who disagree with the policy of the *Gemeinde* or who do not wish to join it. These alternative groupings are especially noticeable in Berlin, a city that has twice the Jewish population of Frankfurt and perhaps as many Jews as all other German cities combined. Alternative groups do, however, exist in other cities such as Cologne, and Jews can simply not join the *Gemeinde* in their town, either praying in their home or not praying at all.

One such alternative to the *Gemeinde* are the neo-Orthodox Jews who insist on strict interpretation of the laws of *Kashruth* (kosher food) as well as all the sexual and hygienic rules found in the *Talmud*, the traditional Jewish teachings. Such congregations were first organized by Jews who disagreed with the ideas and forms of ritual introduced by the "Liberals," who had won the majority of seats on the Frankfurt Jewish Community Council and had also won in other towns. Starting with the *Jeshurun* congregation organized by Rabbi Samuel R. Hirsch in 1875 in Frankfurt, the neo-Orthodox movement soon spread to other cities. The *Adass Jisroel* congregation is the only neo-Orthodox synagogue surviving in Germany, though the ideas of the movement are becoming more widespread again both in Germany and in the United States.

The original *Adass* synagogue was burnt, as were so many others, but the cemetery in Weissensee survived, though overgrown and neglected. Mario Offenberg, a pre-Hitler *Adass* functionary, made a claim for recognition of the rebuilt congregation in the mid-1980s as an alternative *Gemeinde*, an *Austrittsgemeinde*, with full recognition as an independent religious body under German law. He also laid claim to all real estate and other assets formerly owned by the *Adass*. His first appeal was directed to Erich Honecker, the Communist boss of East Germany, since the *Adass* community was located in East Berlin.[1] Offenberg received sufficient political backing in that quarter so that the official East German Museum Education service published a history of the *Adass* congregation written by Offenberg.[2] However, he did not receive recognition as an independent religious community that would be subsidized by government funds. He had to be satisfied with the status of a charitable organization. He also failed to get any of the real estate returned or any other assets. The DDR did not acknowledge itself to be the heir of the German government under Hitler and, therefore, claimed that it was not responsible for the return of anything sequestered by the Nazis. As far as the East German government was concerned, all of its citizens not specifically charged as Nazis were *ipso facto* victims of Nazism. Therefore, nobody was entitled to any special compensation except the small pension given to all survivors of the concentration camps. The fall of Honecker and the Berlin Wall in 1989 forced Offenberg to take his appeal for recognition to the unified but predominantly West German government. He demanded equal status with the regular Berlin *Gemeinde*, a status that the *Adass* had been accorded before Hitler. He was fiercely opposed by Heinz Galinski, speaking both as an individual and as spokesman for the Berlin *Gemeinde*. The opposition was not based on religious grounds but on the fact that the Berlin *Gemeinde* claimed to represent all Jews and that Offenberg was only after financial gain. At present, while the *Adass* has not received status as an official *Gemeinde*, it is a fully functioning congregation that, among other activities, runs the successful Beth Cafe in East Berlin.

In November 1993, the Berlin cultural commission requested an appropriation from the Berlin Senate to support the community activities of the *Adass* congregation. This appropriation passed unanimously. However, the Senate also went on record that it considered the original *Adass* congregation to have been dissolved by the Nazis in 1939 and that therefore the present *Adass* congregation cannot be considered a legal heir to the property of the old *Adass* community.

The *Adass* claims a membership of over 200 members of German Jewish and Russian Jewish origins. It holds regular services and issues a small monthly bulletin. Like many dissident groups, the *Adass* has received support, emotional and political, from the Lauder foundation of New York and from the *Lubavitcher* movement. It is accepted as a regular part of Berlin's Jewish scene.

The earliest of the neo-Orthodox congregations, the *Jeshurun*, has resettled its members in New York City, where it has built up a community that includes synagogue, ritual bath, school, and social services. As an organization it has not returned to Frankfurt, though some of its members have resettled there.

Another group of Jews that must be considered outside the mainstream are the *Lubavitcher Hasidim*, a proselytizing group of Orthodox Jews. *Hasidism* is a movement that began in Poland in the eighteenth century, founded by Rabbi Israel ben Eliezer Baal Shem Tov. The members of the movement stress feeling and emotion in addition to Jewish learning and use song and dancing in their celebrations. *Hasidic* rabbis are reputed to have special powers to bless in addition to great wisdom. Each branch of the movement is named after the town where the founder of the branch held court. The *Lubavitchers* began in a small town in Poland and now have their worldwide headquarters in Brooklyn, New York. The present head, Rabbi Menachem Schneerson, draws his descent from the founder of the group. The *Lubavitcher Hasids* differ from other *Hasidic* groups by actively seeking additional members and sending out graduates from its schools as *Schaliach* (emissaries) who act as missionaries.[3] This group has played a considerable role in the rebuilding of Jewish communities in Germany and in the former Soviet Union. They contacted the East German Jewish groups immediately after the fall of the Communists in 1989 and are active in West Germany as well. They maintain a headquarters for all *Lubavitcher* activity in Europe and publish a German version of their magazine, *Chai* (Life), in Vienna for distribution in Germany, Austria, and Switzerland. There is a *Lubavitch Talmud Torah* study group in Munich and the *Lubavitch* emissary, Rabbi Diskin, is employed by the Jewish *Gemeinde*. Members of the *Lubavitch* group will go anywhere, talk to any Jewish gathering, and offer their considerable Orthodox Jewish learning to those who have forgotten it or who never had any contact with the Eastern European traditions. The *Lubavitch* emissaries follow the Eastern Jewish rather than Western European custom of stressing their role as teachers and advisors rather than as administrators of a congregation. Some of the Russian Jews are more comfortable in this pattern of Jewishness than in the German model. The newly formed Potsdam congregation of Jews from Russia is headed by a *Lubavitch* rabbi, Rabbi Naphtali Greenberg.[4] There is pressure from the "Democratic List" in the Berlin Community Council to hire a *Lubavitch* rabbi to work with the youth groups.

The fact that the very Orthodox Jews, with their black coats and side curls, fit the German conception of how a Jew should look has made it comparatively easy for the *Lubavitcher* and similar groups to find acceptance among the Germans in Germany. When the general German population and, especially, the right-wingers wish to portray a Jew, it is the very-Orthodox they picture. Since the very-Orthodox Jewish groupings are willing to be shown as differing from the Germans in dress, in culture, and in religion, this imaging is very satisfactory to both sides. German and other non-

Orthodox Jews have always been uncomfortable with this portrayal of Jews as a group of "non-Western," cultural outsiders.

Conflict between the very-Orthodox and the mainstream *Gemeinden* became extremely public in the outcry over the construction of a new supermarket on the site of the old Jewish cemetery in Hamburg. The Hamburg *Gemeinde*, considering the cemetery to be desecrated and destroyed during the Hitler era, had transferred the few remaining graves to the new Jewish cemetery. They then sold the old site to a developer in 1950. The proceeds of the sale were primarily devoted to the care of the poor Jews in Hamburg at a time when poverty was widespread among the Jewish community. This agreed with the Jewish admonition that life had the highest priority among the Jewish virtues.

When the developer resold the land during 1991 and a new, larger supermarket was to be built in 1992, a few fragments of human bone were uncovered. The very-Orthodox *Athra Kadisha*, the Defenders of the Jewish Burial Sites, attacked the Hamburg *Gemeinde* for supposed disregard of the Jewish ritual law about the eternal holiness of all Jewish burial sites. This same conflict had already arisen between this group and the government of Israel, with the *Athra Kadisha* charging that the new road projected for Jerusalem would cut through possible Jewish burial sites and objecting to any possible archeological work on the same grounds.

In Hamburg, Orthodox Jews in black coats and wide-brimmed hats came from the United States, Holland, Israel, England, and France to engage in street demonstrations and civil disobedience. German press and TV coverage was extensive.[5] Pictures of these demonstrations continued to appear in later magazines and books, among them a right-wing pamphlet where a picture was titled, "These are Germans?" The issue of the cemetery was finally settled under a compromise arranged by the *Ashkenazi* Rabbi of Jerusalem, but the conflict has not been forgotten. The dispute continues to smoulder between those who would be Orthodox Jews living in any country and those, like Mr. Bubis, who wish to be "German citizens of Jewish faith." To many of the Jews in Germany, this whole affair was simply another instance of the willingness of Jews outside Germany to interfere in German Jewish affairs and to treat the Jews of Germany as second-class Jews. More will be said about this thorny issue in Chapter Seven.

A large number of Israelis living in Germany want nothing to do with the Orthodox Jews or with their ideas. As far as these Israelis are concerned, these Orthodox Jews do not represent Judaism as such; rather, they reflect the traditions that arose in the ghettos of Russia and Poland in the eighteenth and nineteenth centuries. It was in those ghettos of Eastern Europe that the black coats, the wide-brimmed hats, the loud prayers chanted with a rocking motion of the body, and the many other cultural traits immortalized in the books of Martin Buber, the film "Fiddler on the Roof," and the photographic images of Ramon Vishniac originated. These images were romanticized as "old-style Judaism" in the 1940s and 1950s, after the destruction of these communities and are now often presented as the only form of traditional Judaism. This image also includes the endless study of the Torah, which allowed the men to mentally withdraw from the world. The traditions of the *Sephardim*, the Jews who originated in Spain and spread all over the Orient, have only recently been rediscovered by the Jewish museums, and books about this culture are still scarce. At the same time, the traditions of German Jewry, as separate from the culture of the intellectuals driven out by Hitler, is hardly known. Both of these Jewish traditions originated in medieval times, hundreds of years before Russia and Poland became centers of Judaism. These cultural differences within the Jewish minority have often been glossed over, but they do exist and have political consequences within all Jewish communities, including those of Germany and Israel.

The theocratic rules that the very-Orthodox wish to establish over all whom they consider to be true Jews would control all phases of life, including food, daily activities, sex, and the pictures that may be used in advertisements. These are often exactly what these Israelis wished to escape when they left Israel. They may resent even the milder form of Orthodoxy as represented by the practices of the official *Gemeinde*. Sometimes the Israelis also wish to escape the all-Jewish social setting in which they grew up.

Israelis who have children in Germany are the most likely to make their compromises with the *Gemeinde* practices for the sake of Jewish schooling for their children. Many other Israelis remain aloof, which is made easier by their belief that they are just temporary residents in Germany, that they are there for economic reasons, and they will eventually return to Israel. The economic opportunities offered in Germany, even during a recession, are usually much greater than those available in Israel at any time. If peace really comes to the Middle East, Israel may become economically attractive again to both Israelis and Russian Jews living in Germany, and the flow of immigrants might reverse to some extent.

Germany is also Israel's second largest trading partner. The volume is second only to the trade between the United States and Israel. The amount of trade does not include the large sums of money sent by Germany to Israel as reparations. Such a volume of trade offers many opportunities to the Israelis who have come to Germany.

There are a number of Israelis in Germany who are bitterly opposed to the rabbinical controls that exist in Israel and, by extension, to the Orthodox Jews in Germany as well. These are people who have, in one way or another, fallen afoul the Jewish ritual law, which is, in almost all cases, the civil law in Israel as well. Some have been married by Reform rabbis, marriages that are not recognized in Israel. Others have married non-Jews or have found that a non-Jewish parent must be buried in a special, separate section of the cemeteries. Homosexuality is considered to be an abomination by the Orthodox, and the former Chief Rabbi of Britain has even suggested genetic engineering to prevent homosexuality.[6] There are women who have had trouble obtaining their religious divorce papers, the *Get*, without which they cannot remarry according to Jewish law. By *Halachic* rule, the giving of the *Get* is the exclusive prerogative of the husband. This is especially objectionable to today's more liberated women, but it has economic consequences regarding child custody, property settlement, and alimony. All these opponents of Jewish Orthodoxy consider themselves good Jews, but after their experiences with the official Jewish religion, they want no further dealings with any form of Orthodoxy. In part, these opponents of today's Orthodoxy base their beliefs on the Bible, where ordinary people like Job had direct dialog with the Deity and women like Deborah ruled as judges over ancient Israel. Some others denounce rabbis and officials of the community for being allied only to the rich and powerful and for caring nothing about ordinary Jews.

Many of the Russian Jews who are recent arrivals in Germany share some of the social outlook of the Israelis. They, too, prefer the wider economic opportunities in Germany to the more limited chances in Israel. There are those who distrust some of the German and Jewish social agencies that have at times exerted pressure on the Russian emigrés to go to Israel. This is especially true of the academically trained Russian Jews: doctors, physicists, geologists, musicians, and teachers who insisted to us that they did not care to become ditch diggers and taxi drivers in Israel.[7]

The passports of these Russian refugees state unequivocally that these immigrants are Jews by nationality. The passports say nothing about religion since religion was never mentioned on Russian passports. All religion, including the Jewish religion, was forcibly discouraged under the Soviet regime. Any form of religious instruction was forbidden. Therefore, many of the Russian Jews are ignorant of Jewish traditions, ritual law, and Hebrew. As one of the Berlin cantors complained to us: "They don't even know how to *davn*" (pray).[8] Until 1980 Heinz Galinski opposed so many Russian refugees coming to Berlin. "They don't share our culture," he complained; he also deplored the overloading of the Jewish social services by these newcomers.[9] Since then, both he and the *Gemeinde* reversed their attitudes and Russian refugees are now welcomed. It was Galinski who fought against the deportation of Russian Jews to Israel on a number of occasions. However, there still seems to be a certain amount of discrimination, and there are few community functions where Russian or Ukrainian is spoken as the primary language. There are officials of the *Gemeinde* who speak Russian as well as German, but newcomers are strongly urged not only to learn German quickly, but also to become German Jews culturally as well. Of course, it is difficult for Russian Jews, as for any foreigners, to obtain German citizenship. There are a number of proposals before the legislature to alleviate this problem, but they have not become law yet.

The Centrum Judaicum, located in the "New Synagogue" and the Berlin Jewish Museum, occupy ambivalent positions to the *Gemeinde*. The Centrum Judaicum, under Dr. Herrmann Simon, was established in the Communist section of Berlin before the unification of Germany. Its avowed purpose was to give information to Jews and non-Jews about Jewish culture. This would have made it a potent counterbalance to the East Berlin *Gemeinde*. With unification, some of the Centrum's functions are being fulfilled by the *Gemeinde*, and the entire *Orianienburgerstrasse* area where the "New Synagogue" is located has become a center of Jewish activity. There is discussion of whether and how this center should become a part of the *Gemeinde* or stay as an independent foundation. One of the problems is money, since the reconstruction of the "New Synagogue" has been carried out in a fairly lavish style, subsidized by both the Berlin and the Federal German governments. The *Gemeinde* would like to take over this site provided the subsidies continue and would also like to control exactly what kind of "Jewish culture" will be shown.

The Jewish Museum, with a good collection of Jewish ritual silver and paintings by Jewish artists, is part of the Berlin city museum and is under the authority of the Berlin Cultural Ministry. Officially, at least, it has no ties to the *Gemeinde*, although its director is a member and has retained very close relations with the community headquarters at *Fasanenstrasse*. Now that there are plans to build a much larger Jewish museum in Berlin, the questions of administration and policy become even more serious. There are considerable questions about whether such a museum should represent the official version of Judaism or make room for dissident versions of Judaism as well. Certainly, the Jewish Communists and the opponents of Zionism would get short shrift if the *Gemeinde* decides what is to be shown.

The more secular *Jüdischer Kulturverein* (Jewish Cultural Club) offers another alternative to the *Gemeinde*. Everyone is welcome as a member, regardless of whether they are Jews by *Halachic* descent, individuals who consider themselves to be Jews without that ritual authority, or are individuals sincerely interested in Jewish culture. The *Kulturverein* also developed under the DDR and was backed by that government as an alternative to the religiously minded *Gemeinde*. Today, the *Kulturverein* is still vaguely Marxist in orientation, and it has fought for the retention of the street names of anti-Nazi Communists in East Berlin. Members of the *Kulturverein* take a prominent role in anti-right-wing demonstrations.

The *Kulturverein* holds regular Friday night services alternating languages between German and Russian. There is no regular rabbi, but the services might be led by a *Hasid*, a kabbalist, or a visiting rabbi. Women are accepted as equals and sit with the men at the services. The *Kulturverein* also has weekly social get-togethers, musicales, and discussions. Russian and English are used as alternative languages to German, and there is usually someone who does the necessary translating. The club newsletter is issued in German and Russian editions. Contact is maintained with Jewish groups in a number of cities in the former Soviet Union, and the club sends financial help for social as well as religious needs as far as its limited financial resources permit. In the past few years the club has received some subsidies for its social programs from the Berlin Senate, but that funding has now been cut under the new German austerity program. Members of the *Kulturverein* are free to join the *Gemeinde* if they are eligible as well as maintaining their club membership. In the 1993 *Gemeinde* elections, several members of the *Kulturverein* won seats on various committees as part of the "Democratic List," an alliance of various opposition groups to the controlling "Liberals." The consensus is, however, that they will be unable to affect any basic policy change in the *Gemeinde*. They do raise issues to be discussed and help in the changeover to the new generation.

The political and social slot in the Jewish community now occupied by the *Kulturverein* and its allies was formerly held by the Reform Jewish congregations, a movement by Jewish liberals who formulated "Reform Judaism" at the Brunswick conference of 1844. The early Reform movement considered many of the *Talmudic* dietary and hygienic laws irrelevant under modern, Western European conditions, and it tried to define Judaism as a creed with some similarity in scope to the Protestant Christian equivalents. Their Judaism was a religion, not a culture, and even less a nationalism. Later, the sharp divisions between Orthodox and Reform became somewhat blurred with the establishment of "Liberal" and "Conservative" Jewish congregations that filled the void between the two extreme wings of Judaism. The most crucial difference between Reform and Orthodox Judaism is that, among the Reform Jews, descent is reckoned by the father as well as by the mother. Reform congregations are accepted as part of the Jewish community in the United States and England, but they are not recognized in Israel.

When Hitler declared all Jews to be a "race," without reference to belief or religion, the Reform group's attempt to bring Judaism into the German cultural and scientific mainstream collapsed. No Jew was allowed to be a German under Hitler's definition. All Jews, whether Orthodox, Reform, or even baptized, were considered beyond the Pale of German or West European civilizations and suitable only for hard labor or extermination. The effects of this policy on the present Jewish community are the subject of Chapter Four.

The Reform movement has not really been revived in Germany since the end of World War II. Recently, however, Reform congregations have arisen in Russia.[10] It is quite conceivable that Reform Judaism will be reintroduced into Germany from the East. Certainly, the new Jewish study centers now springing up as separate from synagogues might be a starting point for such a development.

In October 1993, Rabbi Alexander M. Schindler of the Union of American Hebrew Congregations (Reform Jews) announced a five-million-dollar program "to reach out to those of our neighbors who have no religion." Commenting on the resistance of Jews to proselytism, both in doing it and receiving such efforts, Rabbi Schindler hearkened back to the Maccabean period in Jewish history in the first and second century B.C.11 Under such a program, support would be available for Reform congregations just as it is for the *Lubavitchers*.

It must be remembered that Reform congregations were members of the *Gemeinden* in Germany even before Hitler. Such a development today would require a considerable readjustment by the *Gemeinden* and the *Zentralrat*; failure to do so would leave a considerable number of those who consider themselves Jews outside the formal Jewish structure, not only by choice but by necessity.

Another group of Jewish dissidents that must be mentioned are the German Jewish anti-Zionists. They are exemplified by Michael Wolffsohn, professor at the *Bundeswehr* (military) University. He and a group of other Jews believe that they are patriotic Germans of Jewish religion, no different from other Germans who belong to other religions. They oppose the viewpoint that all Jews must be Zionists. To them, the State of Israel represents no part of Jewish culture but is an artificial creation serving the political objective of some Jews. They consider that Israel as a state was totally destroyed by the Romans in 73 A.D. and that Judaism since has maintained itself strictly as a religious group. They maintain that the Jews of Germany must stop thinking of themselves as people with Israeli and German citizenship, and they blame Zionism and Zionists for much of the hostility that faces the Jews in Germany today. Of course they do not condone in any way the neo-Nazi violence taking place in Germany. Like the Marxists, this group distinguishes between anti-Semitism, which they reject, and anti-Zionism, with which they agree. They do not object to the existence of Israel; they object to it occupying the central role for Jews worldwide.

German patriotism among the Jews in Germany has a long tradition. Strong German nationalism flourished among German Jews, particularly during and after World War I. Memorials to the fallen Jewish heroes of that war were common among the memorials on the walls in many synagogues in Germany.

About 100,000 Jews served in the German armed forces in World War I. Twelve thousand were killed at the front lines. After the war the veterans formed the League of German Front Line Fighters (*Reichsbund Jüdischer Frontsoldaten*) and fought against the postwar propaganda that the Jews had avoided front-line service and were simply war profiteers. It was impossible for these veterans to believe that the comrades with whom they had shared life in the trenches for four years would now turn against them. When Hitler established the Honor Cross for Frontline Fighters (*Ehrenkreuz für Frontkampfer*), many Jews applied for and received this medal. Some Jews continued to wear their World War I medals even in the ghettos of Lodz and Theresienstadt. Today, militant patriotism and nationalism are out of fashion in much of the Western World, and it is hard for the younger generation of Jews to give any respect to this attitude by much of the German Jewish population.

The largest group of dissidents—if that is what they can be called—are the secular Jews without any official Jewish affiliation. These include many of the Jewish intellectuals as well as large numbers of just plain citizens. Judaism, to them, is a tradition and a set of ethics that are part of their lives. They do not need to parade it like the yellow Star of David that the Jews were compelled to wear during the Hitler era. They may have family gatherings for Passover or fast on the Day of Atonement or they may not. They do not recognize any rabbinical authority and feel that their Jewishness is governed only by their own consciences. They are Jews by background and do not deny their Jewishness, but they do not make it the center of their daily lives. This was the viewpoint of many of the returnees to the DDR who wanted to participate in the rebuilding of a new, peaceful Germany. Many of them were Marxists first and Jews second. This attitude that sees an intellectual and secular rather than a religious Judaism has many followers in Germany today.

There are also many Jews who do not care to join the *Gemeinde* for a variety of other reasons. They cannot be considered dissidents at all but are nonmembers of the Jewish communities. Some of them find the fees for membership excessive for the benefits received from the *Gemeinde*. Other Jews are afraid to appear on any list that might connect them with the Jewish minority or even to receive mail from any Jewish organization. The fears created by memories of the Nazi period are very strong and governments are known to have long memories. After all, the German government just convicted Edward Mielke, head of the feared East German secret police, for the supposed murder of two policemen who were killed in 1931. During the height of the right-wing violence in 1992, there were a number of members of the *Kulturverein* who asked to have their copies of the club newsletter sent to them in plain wrappers.[12] The club discussed this proposal but decided that it was more important not to appear to yield to any threat, real or imagined, than to reassure its frightened members.

The number of Jews in each of these dissident groups is hard to determine. The organized dissident groups probably number no more than a thousand people. The size of the group of unaffiliated Jews is quite large, possibly as large as the total membership in the *Gemeinden*. They would not show up adequately in any census since there is no obligation to list religious preference on the form. It is impossible therefore to do more than guess at their number. This, however, brings us to the question of defining whom we consider to be a Jew. For the purposes of this study, we will define as a Jew all those who consider themselves to be Jews or who are so defined by the majority of the German population. As has been clearly shown a number of times in history, under political pressure the nonaffiliated Jew, the half-Jew, and even those who converted to other religions but are of recent Jewish descent are treated as Jews by the majority population and, therefore, must be treated as Jews in an anthropological study. Whether religious groups of all shades use the same standard to define Jewish minority members is not relevant here.

The faults or weaknesses of any individual Jew included in this minority, as we have defined it, are attributed to all Jews. This is as true of the sins of Albert Nachman, the former head of the *Zentralrat*, who was found to have absconded with millions of dollars of Jewish reparation funds that he diverted into his private Swiss bank accounts, as it is of Gregor Gysi and Andre Brie, leading members of the Party for Democratic Socialism. Their viewpoints have often been attributed to their "Jewish background." It is the JEWS, in capital letters, who are blamed, collectively, by some Germans for any real or imagined sins committed by any member of this minority. The religious membership or belief does not enter in this consideration. The Jews also hold all Jews, dissidents or members of the *Gemeinde*, to a higher standard of behavior than they do members of the majority. They criticize anyone who is believed to have brought "discredit to the Jews." Such attitudes are typical of minorities anywhere.

NOTES

1. According to Professor Klaus Herrmann of Concordia University, Montreal, the correspondence between Offenberg and Honecker can be found in the *Arbeitskreis Religion*, Central Committee of the Socialist Unity Party, East German files available in Berlin. Personal communication.

2. Mario Offenberg, *Adass Jisroel: Vernichtet und Vergessen* (Berlin: DDR, Museumspädagogischer Dienst 1986).

3. *Interview with Rav Israel Diskin* in "Jews Week" (Munich: Youth Center of the Israelite Cultural Community, Summer 1993).

4. Correspondence and conversation with Rabbi Hershel Gluck, Chabad Lubavitch, London 1993.

5. Among others, *Jewish Week* (New York: 6 Sept. 1991) and *Hamburger Abendblatt* (24 Oct. 1991). For a full review, see Arie Goral-Sternheim *Mahnung und Menetekel* in "Juden und Deutsche" (*Spiegel*, Special Number, August 1992).

6. *Jewish Chronicle* (London: 26 Aug. 1993).

7. Interviews, Hessenwinckel Refugee Camp, Berlin, June 1991.

8. Interview, Berlin 1990.

9. *New York Times* (25 Sept. 1980). For later attitude, see Andreas Nachama and Julius H. Schoeps, *Aufbau Nach Dem Untergang* (Berlin: Argon Verlag, 1992).

10. Walter Ruby, *A Proud New Breed of Jewish Russians* in "Jewish World" (New York: 19–25 Mar. 1993).

11. *New York Times* (24 Oct. 1993).

12. *Jüdische Korrespondenz* (Berlin: Dec. 1992).

Chapter Three

A Community of Displaced Persons

very Jew in Germany over the age of forty-five has spent part of his or her life in a country other than Germany. They have been in exile from the land of their birth, they have spent time in a labor or displaced person camp, they have been on the run from authority, or they have experienced any combination of these circumstances. The same pattern, minus only the violence, is true for many of the Jews under the age of forty-five as well. Leafing through the October issue of the *Berliner Umschau*, the newspaper of the Berlin Jewish community, accurately reflects this widespread dislocation. Peter Ambros, the press officer, is from Bratislava. Dr. Rachel Salamander, founder and director of the Jewish bookshops in Munich and Berlin, was born in a displaced persons camp in Bavaria. The two youthful chess champions are from Uzbekistan and Odessa, respectively. The author, Michael Wolffsohn, was born in Israel, and so on. Individuals such as these cannot but lack the experience of a stable background and surroundings that are considered the norm in much of the Western World. The terms homeland, patriotism, lifelong friendships, family traditions, and festivals can have little or no meaning in a society where the majority of its population has experienced long periods of such instability. Instability extends to the small things in life as well as the big ones. The "Jewish delicatessen" that is so familiar in New York is actually based on the food of Eastern Europe, especially Romania. The Jew of German origin knows little of pastrami or gefilte fish. One of the Jews from the DDR mourned the loss of the plain, unsugared cornflakes she had been used to and that were no longer obtainable after the German reunification. To her, these cornflakes characterized all of the small, familiar things she had been used to. Yet any community must have a joint set of values, language, and viewpoints if we are to define its members as part of a group instead of as a series of individuals. In order to define the Jews of Germany as a minority, we must show how this diverse individual background and history of instability has been used and combined with present conditions to create such a joint set of values and behavior for the Jews in Germany.

Again Mr. Bubis's life history can serve as an example of the histories of many of the Jews in Germany today.[1] He was born in the German city of Breslau, which is now the Polish city of Wroclaw. When he was eight years old, in 1935, his family fled from Breslau to Deblin in prewar Poland where his grandparents lived. While Poland was undoubtedly familiar to Mr. Bubis's parents who had only left it in 1919, it must have represented a different and alien culture to the young man. The economic condition of the family deteriorated with the move. His brother died of appendicitis. His house was not only smaller, but the conditions in a small Polish town and the large German city of Breslau are totally different. Four years after his displacement to Poland, the Germans and Russians invaded Poland. A brother and sister fled into the Soviet-occupied part of Poland where they disappeared, as did so many other Polish Jews. His mother died in the Bubis family home, but in February 1941 all the Jews in Deblin had to move into that town's ghetto. This was followed by the construction of a labor camp and the beginning of transporting Jews from the West to Deblin and from

Deblin to the extermination camps. Among the transportees was Mr. Bubis's father. At the same time there were also mass executions of Jews. Ignatz Bubis survived, working as a mailman for the ghetto. He was the only survivor of his entire family.

Deblin was a small camp of only 800 Jews. Other camps such as Nevergamme, a labor camp near Hamburg, or Auschwitz, where Heinz Galinski slaved, were even worse. All of these camps were an environment for which the term "unstable" can only be considered a vast understatement. The many published descriptions of life in these camps show that only those individuals survived who did not form strong bonds with fellow workers or supervisors, whether Jews, political prisoners, or German guards. Your fellows could be transported elsewhere suddenly, an outside group of guards could be brought in, or a plot or a method of obtaining illegal food could be betrayed. Death was equally random. A group of female prisoners, already at the door of the gas ovens with their heads shaved, were suddenly reprieved by an order for 300 workers to be sent to Hamburg to clear rubble caused by bombing. A series of blocks in a ghetto were surrounded and everybody found in them shot. Those who were away on errands had a chance of surviving. Anne Frank and her sister died only two months before their camp was liberated. In many cases, those who survived could assign no reason why they lived while so many others died. Psychologists have found that survivors of disasters must deal with feelings of guilt that they survived.

Conditions in Poland did not improve much after the war. In 1946 there were violent anti-Semitic outbreaks, including a pogrom that killed at least fifty Jews in the town of Kielce. Ignatz Bubis records the anti-Semitic attitude of even the leader of the Polish underground, both during the war and after. After the war was over, Ignatz Bubis went back to Germany, dealing first in horses and later in jewelry, currency, and art objects. He had spent a short time in a displaced persons camp near Berlin but did not stay in the camp. This was the period when Zionist groups in the camps exerted strong pressure on every Jew to sign up to go to Israel.[2] Bubis chose to stay in Germany instead of emigrating. Eventually, he became a successful businessman, married, had a daughter, and settled in Frankfurt, where he was elected head of the Frankfurt *Gemeinde*. The same skills that had served the Jewish peddlers for generations, now used in peddling in jewelry and real estate, had made Mr. Bubis wealthy. That wealth, however, exposed him to attacks by the Left, most publicly by the dramatist R. W. Fassbinder. The play "Garbage, the City and Death" included some anti-Jewish lines as well as an attack on speculators, especially Jewish speculators. Bubis and a group of his associates counterfeited tickets and occupied the stage to prevent the performance. When the civic officials asked Bubis how he could oppose the police regulations, he answered, "I have left Germany before, if needful I will do so again."[3] Today, Ignatz Bubis titles his autobiography "I am a German Citizen of Jewish Faith." His name was recently put forward as a suitable candidate for the office of President of Germany by the German weekly, *Die Welt*,[4] an honor that he declined. Yet a local politician in Rostock commented that Mr. Bubis must consider Israel his homeland because he is a Jew.[5] The statement borders on the ridiculous, but it points up the instability in the life of even the spokesman for the Jews in Germany.

The background of Irene Runge, one of the leaders of the *Kulturverein*, is hardly more stable though her life was less threatened. She was born in the United States of German-Jewish parents. The language of her childhood was English. In 1949 her parents decided to return to the German Democratic Republic. In that Communist state, the American ideals of rugged individualism and capitalist democracy were held up to scorn, and Zionism was not mentioned at all. The individual was expected to subordinate his or her needs to the needs of the State. On the other hand, the State would take care of most problems of living.[6] In 1989 the DDR and all it stood for disappeared—suddenly and unexpectedly—from the German scene. What had been East German patriotism became, retroactively, treason and the betrayal of associates.[7] Irene Runge lost her position because of her political activism. Her Jewishness, which had been downplayed under the Communists, now became a positive attribute and her participation in Jewish religious affairs has increased. Instability in her life is what she shares with Mr. Bubis.

The same reversals of values and circumstances are also often true for many of the more recent immigrants to Germany. Jews in the Soviet Union in the last several decades risked a visit by the secret police if they taught their children about the Jewish religion or the Hebrew language. Yiddish was recognized as the "national language" of the Jews in Russia, but the instruction in Hebrew was strongly discouraged if not considered "antirevolutionary." A number of Jews were imprisoned or executed because of their Jewishness in the so-called Jewish doctors' plot in Russia in 1952. Now their fellow Jews in Germany look down on some of the Russian refugees because they did not initiate their children into all the Jewish traditions. Under Communism the way to get ahead in the Soviet system was to conform. Now the emphasis is on individual initiative and "doing your own thing."

As citizens of the Soviet Union, many Russian Jews fought against the Germans in what was called the "Great Patriotic War" (1941–1945) or they were victims of starvation during the German siege of Leningrad. Those who lived in western Russia were forced to flee from the advancing German armies. Those who did not flee or did not flee fast enough died as the execution squads (*Sonderkommando*) systematically wiped out all the Jews they could find. Now the same Russian Jews who fled from the Germans are pressured by circumstances not only to learn the German language but to adopt German culture. The homeland these Russian Jews grew up in has not only changed the value system they knew but, in some cases, has changed even the name and nationality of their home towns.[8] The instability of their life was increased further by the fact that these refugees from Russia often arrived in Germany with only as many personal possessions as could be packed into one suitcase. On arrival in Germany they were sent to a refugee camp which differed little or not at all from the displaced persons camps of fifty years earlier. Almost invariably such camps are located in barracks of the armed forces, now surplus, as they were just after the end of World War II. They are almost always located away from the center of town and they lack public transportation from camp to city. Registering for a job, visiting a sick relative in the hospital, or attending school required an all-day expedition and threading one's way through an unfamiliar bureaucracy.[9] It is not surprising if the emigrés from Russia, like the Holocaust survivors, have trouble feeling a sense of "belonging" even after they leave the camps. Learning the language well enough to function in it is relatively easy. Learning to joke in it, learning the German social forms and expected behavior is much harder. Then there are the little things that are so important to a sense of "home," such as shifting from tea served from a samovar to serving German-style afternoon coffee.

The Israelis in Germany have seen their homeland evolve very far from the religious vision of a "Holy Land" and from the idealistic Zionism of Theodor Herzl and his associates. Many of the *kibbutzim* that were the symbol of Israel in 1948 have disappeared, have turned themselves into corporations with shares listed on the stock exchange, or have lost their importance. The present-day Israel must deal with the very practical ideas and problems of urban sprawl, economic competition on a worldwide scale, and crime. Many Israelis have had personal experience with open warfare or with the Arab terrorism of the Arab-Israeli conflict, experiences that do not promote a sense of stability. The Israelis are living in the country—Germany—whose name has been made synonymous with the greatest crime against the Jews in history. The fellow refugees with whom they share their fear of a Nazi revival are Turks, followers of the same Muslim religion as the Arabs. It is difficult for the Israelis in Germany, as it is for so many other Jews, to define their "proper" role in Germany and a value system in which they can feel comfortable.

The German Jews who have returned to Germany know that they and their parents spent the war years as exiles in the United States,

England, the Dominican Republic, Shanghai, or Moscow. They must now forget both the language and the culture that they had adopted and become, once more, German Jews in the land where their relatives had been driven to their death. For them, too, it is difficult to find a "proper" role for themselves.

Instability taught most of the Jews one particular quality. All of them learned to seize opportunities quickly, regardless of whether these opportunities dealt with a piece of bread, a good financial deal, or escape from the agents of a dictatorial and arbitrary regime. They also learned to suppress their feelings about their fellow men, at least publicly, and to mask their feelings when dealing with authorities.

Since there are so few traditional norms and no natural joint heritage to fall back on among the diverse individuals who consti-tute the community of Jews in Germany, new norms must be adopted if that community is to function as a unit. What is needed is either a Jewish or a German value system or a synthesis of the two to meet the needs and be accepted by the majority of the members of the community.

The consensus that seems to be developing among the Jews of Germany is a culture somewhat similar to that of the urban German Jews prior to 1933. The traditions that served intellectuals such as Albert Einstein and Kurt Tucholsky, businessmen like Emil Rathenau, the Mosse and Ullstein families, and the many small storekeepers and workers is both socially acceptable and economi-cally feasible today. The tradition is very flexible; it allows room for observant Jews, secular Jews, and Marxists. It is also relatively free from ethnocentrism, allowing room for German Jews, Eastern Jews, and the many groupings that fit neither classification. It also provides for the absorption of many different nationalities into a German milieu.

Naturally this heritage is a construct, ignoring many facts of the history of the Jews in Germany and emphasizing others. Many things must be forgotten or ignored so that this consensus can become the accepted culture of the Jews in Germany as they are today. Things that are deemphasized today include many of the special foods and beverages that characterized the difference between "Eastern" and "German" Jews. The old Yiddish terminology and phrases and jokes that were part of daily conversation are no longer heard and the standard German clothing of today has replaced the distinctive dress of Jews in Russia and Poland. In 1933 one-third of all the Jews living in Berlin held Polish rather than German passports. The same was true in Leipzig and in many other cities of Germany. These Eastern Jews, who were residents but not citizens of Germany, spoke Yiddish as their mother tongue. They were primarily marginal industrial workers and craftsmen. Many were Orthodox in religion or were *Hasidim*. Others were Marxists, many of them members of the *Bund*, the *Allgemeiner Yiddischer Arbeiter Bund*, an organization that had arisen around the turn of the century in Poland. Among the Yiddish speakers in Germany were poets who wrote in Yiddish and there was an active Yiddish theater. Many Jews of Eastern European background were active in the German artistic world without ever being fully accepted as German Jews. Most German Jews considered the Eastern European Jews as socially inferior to both Spanish and German Jews, regardless of whether they came from Lithuania, Poland, Hungary, Bessarabia, or Russia. Even among the Eastern Jews there were additional social divisions. Jews who originated in Silesia or East Prussia, part of Germany during the days of the Empire before World War I, were often considered *Wasser Polacken* (watered down Poles) and were considered not quite German Jews. Certainly the family of Heinz Galinski, the long-time head of the Berlin community after World War II, would not have been acknowledged as German Jews and, in some circles, still would not be today. Among most Jews, all those whose families were formerly resident in Germany are classified as *Yekkes*, a derogatory term that includes Austrian Jews as well.[10]

Another group of German Jews has also suffered a loss of their history and traditions. These were the *Landjuden*, country or village Jews whose communities were found primarily in the Rhineland,

Würtemberg, Baden, and Silesia. These were communities of Orthodox Jews whose families had been settled in these villages for centuries. Most of them were small-scale traders in farm products, cattle and horses, grain, home-woven linens, and duck and goose feathers. There were also Jewish peddlers, who sold ribbons, pots, and other manufactured goods to the peasants, Jews and Christians alike. These peddlers often served as neutral arbiters since they had no ties to a particular faction of the village.[11] From these trading activities it is only a small step to becoming bakers, butchers, storekeepers, or small-scale manufacturers. Since trading requires cash, some Jews also became small-scale bankers. This is the origin of such wealthy banking families as the Rothschilds and the Mendelsohns. Members of these successful families moved to the cities, particularly Frankfurt, Berlin, and Dresden, but most of the *Landjuden* remained in their small towns and villages. Only a few pamphlets or books of local historians remind us of these groups today.

These rural communities of Jews were as much victims of the industrial and commercial trends of the twentieth century as they were of the Holocaust. The drift from the villages to the big cities was already well under way in the 1920s and 1930s, but the Nazis destroyed all who were left of these village Jews. It might be possible for a Jew to hide among the anonymous crowds in cities like Frankfurt or Berlin. There was no hiding place in the villages where everybody knew everybody. There were always enough Nazis or people who hoped to gain economically from the destruction of the Jews to denounce them and have their property seized and their persons threatened. The fact that Jewish families had lived in peace with their Christian neighbors for centuries offered no protection.

Many of the rural synagogues and ritual-bath buildings have survived both the Holocaust and the war. They stand, often well maintained, as monuments to a departed way of life. Occasionally, they are visited by an elderly Jewish former resident of the village returning for sentiment's sake to their old homes from overseas.

The synagogues in some of the smaller cities such as Erlangen or Lubeck are utilized for services a few times a year, but there has been no large resident congregation. The Lübeck congregation has twenty-one members today. In March, 1994 the synagogue was damaged by a firebomb presumed to be hurled by a right-wing extremist. Until now these services were a political gesture to remind the Germans of the former presence of Jews in their communities. Now a few of these towns are being resettled by new Jewish groups of suburbanites or other new-comers whose traditions are not part of the heritage of these towns. The new congregation of Potsdam, Russian Jews with a *Lubavitcher* rabbi, is an example of such resettlement. Certainly the present congregation is not part of the royal and conservative tradition of Potsdam. The existence of an old Jewish cemetery or a former synagogue may, however, form a bridge between the old and the new Jewish communities. This has been the case in the city of Magdeburg, where the new congregation of Russian Jews is building on a foundation of a 1000-year-old tradition, an old Jewish cemetery and a few German Jewish survivors. As in many of the new congregations, funding and housing present major problems for long-term growth.

In some German cities, Jews dominated a certain trade or occupation. This was the case in Leipzig, where the fur trade was almost totally in Jewish hands. The Jews were the dealers and the processors. From Leipzig, in the old days, traders travelled every year to the great fur markets to the east, Nizhy-Novgorod, Vladivostok, and other cities. The furs were brought back to Leipzig to be sorted and sewn into coats, scarves and jackets. The Leipzig Jewish community had strong ties to Eastern Europe. These ties go back for centuries, a fact documented by the lithographs of the Leipzig "Messe" or fair in 1836 showing the arrival of Jews in traditional dress from the East.[12] The surviving synagogue in Leipzig is named for the Galician trading town of Grodny, Poland, but the fur workers have almost all disappeared from Leipzig. Many of them moved to 30th Street in New York. The old fur dealers' district in Leipzig, the

Brühl, survives only as a tourist attraction. The small, present-day Jewish community may be able to build on the old traditions, but it will be a long time indeed until they can be said to "feel at home" in Leipzig.

In Berlin there is an attempt to restore the old high-fashion dress industry that was almost completely in Jewish hands before Hitler. A consortium that includes Jews from Israel, the United States, and France is planning to build a large fashion center near the old ghetto. Their task of assembling the large plot of real estate was made easier by the fact that the area was covered by reparations claims that the new investors bought. At the same time, the Jewish community is sponsoring lectures about the Berlin fashion industry of the past, and a book dealing with that history has been issued by a private publisher. However, many of the firms that will be recruited to occupy this center are not Jewish, and the Jewish history, according to the sponsors, will not be emphasized in the center once it is built. Again, we will have a new institution that draws on old traditions to give it a historical base.

The Oriental rug dealers of Hamburg are also in a good position to capitalize on an old tradition. Originally all this trade was in the hands of Bokharans, Sephardic Jews from what is now Uzbekistan. Their numbers were reenforced after World War II by a group of Iranian Jews fleeing from the fundamentalist Islamic revolution in their country. Until now this group of Sephardic Jews has been fairly isolated from the mainstream *Ashkenazic* Hamburg Jewish community, but the numbers of Oriental Jews in Hamburg are increasing with refugees from Tadjikistan, Kazakhstan, and Uzbek-istan, regions that have been becoming increasingly Islamic since their separation from the Soviet Union. It is unlikely that these Jews will blend in well with the Hamburg *Gemeinde* unless the Hamburg Jewish community follows the lead of the Vienna community and establishes a "Bokharan" congregation. Such a development would add another element to the diversity of the Jews in Germany.

It is the unstable and diverse background of the Jews in Germany that gives the *Gemeinden* their tremendous psychological importance. One may be against the *Gemeinde* policy, one may refuse to join the *Gemeinde*, but it is the *Gemeinde* that furnishes the yardstick against which all other Jewish positions can be measured. Without the *Gemeinde* there could be Jews living in Germany, but it would not be a group of people that could be characterized as a Jewish minority with its own social structure.

The existence of the State of Israel as a political entity plays a similar role in Jewish thinking as does the existence of the *Gemeinde*. It provides both a norm and a reassurance for most of the Jews of Germany. It is the final refuge "If the worst comes to the worst," a place where Jews are in the majority and in power and where all Jews are welcome. This is probably one of the reasons why Zionism is such a major feature in most of the Jewish activities in Germany. This attitude has nothing to do with approval or disapproval for any of the policies of whatever government is in power in Israel and still less with any real plans to resettle there. It is the safety net that Israel represents that is important, not its policies. Israel is a potential refuge or even a safe burial ground to a population that feels it has neither safety nor a secure resting place. For this safety net, the Jews are willing to expend both cash and political capital.

To a much lesser extent the United States fills a similar role as does Israel, as a potential refuge in case of trouble. On a practical basis, the United States would be the preferred place to flee to, but the Jews know the tight restrictions and long delays in obtaining a visa. This lessens its value in cases of emergency, as the memories of the failure of the United States to admit refugees in 1939–1941 show everyone. The other respects in which both Israel and the United States have an impact on the Jews in Germany will be discussed in Chapter Seven.

If we accept these parameters of the existence of a consensus of culture among the Jews in Germany, just what kind of a cultural community has arisen there? The common language of this community is German, not Yiddish or Hebrew. The German that is spoken among the Jews can be considered more of a *lingua franca* than a mother tongue. Only a small percentage of the Jewish

German speakers are familiar with the German literary classics or the German legends and folk tales. The culture of the Jewish community is also an urban culture, since it is in the cities that both economic opportunity and fellow Jews can be found. It is a culture where the families of the individual Jew can be widely scattered geographically. These were patterns that already existed to some extent among the German Jews of the 1930s and exist today among the more recent immigrants and returnees. Jews in Germany may have relatives in Jerusalem or New York, in St. Petersburg or Johannesburg. Siblings, even if geographically separated, are often bound to each other by personal or even business ties. Their children drift apart from their cousins, separated by distance and life experiences. Some contact and family connection is usually maintained between the cousins with congratulatory cards or condolences, as appropriate, and by international phone calls. Perhaps one reason for keeping up these contacts is "because one never knows where one ends up."

Most of the Jews in Germany have another characteristic in common: They do not feel safe in Germany or, for that matter, they do not feel safe anywhere. This has created what has been called the "sitting on one packed suitcase" syndrome.[13] If things get too bad, is the belief, one can always move somewhere else. This syndrome makes it unlikely that the Jews in Germany will develop a deep commitment in the near future to any material object or long-term project, social or political. Relationships with other persons are more likely to be with a wide group of casual acquaintances than deep ones with a few close friends or relatives. Beautiful objects, apartments, or comfortable surroundings are enjoyed but not necessarily considered permanent. "Nothing I have here, neither my six room apartment, my offices, my car or my stocks mean anything to me," Fritz is quoted.[14] Others have voiced similar sentiments in conversation with us. This does not mean, however, that the Jews in Germany do not have strong feelings about certain issues or do not love beautiful things. Fritz loves his practice of law. Gregor Gysi certainly gives the impression that he is attached to his political philosophy and has indeed made considerable sacrifices for it, but there is less feeling of building for the next generation among the Jews in Germany than there had been in the past. The pre-1933 German Jews were, by and large, believers that things could be changed for the better, that existing evils could disappear. Very little of that optimism is evident today. There is much more of a belief in fighting so that things do not get worse. Of course this belief is true among many non-Jews in Germany as well.

Many Jews, individually and as members of the Jewish community, take strong political stands. The leaders of the *Gemeinde* were prominent in the front of the demonstrations that protested the death of the Turks killed by neo-Nazis in Solingen in June 1993. Many Jews are active in politics, but despite this activity, there is little total commitment of time and resources that marked the Marxists, among others, in the 1930s. Cynicism guards against the disappointments and betrayals that were so much a feature of the political past. Charismatic leaders of all kinds are strongly discounted today.

There is one kind of material possession that is highly valued among today's Jews. Pictures and books are kept for sentiment's sake and are valued above almost anything else. The number of photographs that have been preserved showing hometowns or family members is almost incredible. This is as true of the Russian refugees as it is among the German Jews. Even the ghettos established during the Holocaust have been preserved in photographs, at the risk of the photographers' lives. Book that are preserved rank slightly behind photographs in numbers and in sentimental value. They include prayer books, novels, philosophy, science, and childrens' books. These do not represent a financial value, although many have that as well, so much as a very personal value. These fragile but easily portable pieces of memory seem to substitute for actual visits to the family or hometowns, families or towns that may no longer exist or that are difficult to visit. The photographs and the books remain together with often strongly romanticized memories of the old days.[15]

The wide range of geographic backgrounds and experiences of the Jews now living in Germany do not necessarily represent drawbacks to the Jewish communities in Germany. In many cases this variety can have economic advantages. There are very few places in the world today where one cannot find someone among one's fellow Jews who know the place or can give an introduction to someone living there. The lack of a concept of homeland or permanence is an advantage for those who deal in international economics.

The culture we have outlined of the Jews in Germany is still only a thin veneer on top of other cultures. This new veneer may be thickening somewhat now that a post-Holocaust and post-immigrant generation is coming of age. But the thinness of this layer of joint culture today can be exemplified, for instance, if one wished to recommend a library for Jewish children in Germany. The tales of Sholom Aleichem of *stedl* life do not touch a common nerve. Andersen's and Grimm's fairy tales are familiar only to the children of a Central European background. The German tales written by Erich Kastner or Karl May, long standard juvenile fare in Germany, seem strange and dated to many Jews. The parents and grandparents of the Jewish children had stranger adventures, if they could be convinced to tell them to their grandchildren. Jewish children will probably long identify with the stories of the Holocaust, the "Diary of Anne Frank," or the story of the Warsaw Ghetto uprising.

Stores of commonplace, normal life of the past are possibly the hardest for Jewish children to identify with. Only Jews over the age of sixty can tell the present generation of a time when everyday, peaceful life was a reality for the Jews of Russia, Poland, or Germany. However, such a life-style, free of upheaval, must be re-created among the young Jews in Germany before we can speak of a stable community.

Past instability and the tentative common culture of the Jews in Germany has other consequences as well. The community has very few tools of social control of its members at its disposal. There are no agreed-upon standards of how members of this minority ought to behave in various circumstances. The only rule that seems to be universal is that individual Jews should not make themselves conspicuous. Ethics in economics, group behavior, and social customs are still left to the individual conscience. Ostracism and social criticism within the group, potent tools in the past for bringing deviants into line, are either ineffective or nonexistent. Behavior is an area that will have to develop gradually among the Jews of Germany, as it has among most minorities.

Another unexplored area of necessary consensus is the status of women. In the Orthodox Jewish tradition women are equal in status but physically separated from the men. This separateness is exemplified by the physical separation in the synagogue and in the ritual bath. The women of the house recite the blessings over the lighting of the Sabbath candles, but the men lead in the observance of Passover in the home and prayers in the synagogue. It was the men who went to the synagogue to study and discuss the *Talmud*.

In the kibbutz in Israel, in the Socialist societies of Russia and the DDR, as well as in much of the modern, capitalist world, the role of women is not only equal but often identical with that of men, of course with the exception of child-bearing. Their occupations are identical, men and women serve in combat in the armed forces, and men and women share in child-rearing and household management. This is a problem, not only for the Jews in Germany, but for traditional cultures all over the world.

NOTES

1. Ignatz Bubis, with Edith Kohn, *Ich bin ein Deutscher Staatsbürger Jüdischen Glaubens* (Koln: Kiepenheuer & Witsch, 1993).

2. Wolfgang Jacobmeyer, *Die Lager der Jüdischen Displaced Person* in "Jüdisches Leben in Deutschland Seit 1945" (Frankfurt: Atheneen Verlag, 1988).

3. Bubis, p. 161.

4. *Germany Considers Jew as President, New York Times* (27 Mar. 1993).

5. There was worldwide coverage of this incident in October 1992.

6. Robin Ostow, *Jews in Contemporary East Germany* (London: Macmillan, 1989) and subsequent personal interviews.

7. Marcus Wolff and others were put on trial and convicted in Germany in 1993 for acts committed while they were officials of the DDR, acts now considered treasonous to Germany.

8. Sverdlov has been changed back to Ektarienburg and Leningrad back to St. Petersburg, among many other place-name changes. At the same time, there are restored, independent nations such as Lithuania and Latvia, as well as brand-new countries such as Moldova and Kazakhstan to say nothing of unrecognized units like Trans-Dniester.

9. In visiting Hessenwinckel camp outside Berlin, as guests of a resident, we were told that we should have obtained prior permission from the central office three miles away. We managed to "sweet-talk" our way in but only because we were Americans.

10. *Yekkes*, or "jackets," described German Jews in Israel who wore ties and jackets and preferred not to engage in physical or agricultural labor.

11. The author's great-grandfather was such a peddler in Bohemia and earned the sobriquet "the Wise" for his advice and arbitration skills.

12. Georg Emanuel Opiz, *Ein Zeichner der Leipziger Messe*. Lithographs reissued by Leipziger Messeamt (DDR) 1986.

13. Wolfgang Benz, *Sitzen auf Gepackten Koffer* in "Juden und Deutsche" (*Spiegel*, Special Number Two, Aug. 1992).

14. Peter Sichrovsky, ed., *Strangers in Their Own Land* (New York: Basic Books, 1986).

15. Romanticized memories were a problem in obtaining the life histories of elderly Jewish emigrants in Washington Heights, New York City. See Michael Cohn, *From Germany to Washington Heights* (New York: Yeshiva University Museum, 1987).

Chapter Four

The Legacy of the Third Reich

Hitler's Third Reich drew a thick, black line through the flow of Jewish history everywhere, especially through the flow of history of the Jews in Germany. Numerically, German Jews made up only a small proportion of the total number of victims of the Holocaust. The best guess is that some 125,000 German Jews died, of a total of some six million Jewish dead. That is about half of all the German Jews alive in 1933. But it was in Germany that the horror developed, step by step. It was in Germany that the Nazis perfected the process of denationalization, degradation, deportation, and mass murder that was later carried out all over Europe. It is in Germany that one finds all the history and symbols that represent the process known to us today as the Holocaust.

The Holocaust, the *Shoah* or the burning, involved more than the killing of six million Jews. Killing of innocents is part of all wars and many ideological or nationalistic movements. During the twentieth century it happened to the Armenians in Turkey; today it is happening in the former Yugoslavia. It is quite possible that Stalin's various purges killed as many people as did Hitler's followers. It is the cold-blooded, scientific attempt to exterminate all that represented Jewish culture, as well as the attempt to kill all persons who had any Jewish blood in their veins in all places where German guns governed, that makes this event almost unique in history.[1]

We must examine the legacy of this period in history as it affects both Jew and German if we are to attempt to understand the status and role of the Jews in Germany today.

Between 1933 and 1938 the Jewish community in Germany was systematically stripped of its role in German society, its total economic and political status. The German Jews were denationalized, made stateless and outlaw, a pattern that had previously existed only in regard to Romanies and heretics in medieval Europe. They were no longer German Jews or Polish Jews, they were simply Jews. If they were allowed to play music, it was only Jewish music that was allowed them. If they were allowed to watch theater, it was only Jewish theater. All contacts between Jews and non-Jews were interdicted, not only prohibited, but made physically impossible. The Nazis made every effort to render the Jews invisible as people. In addition to this, all Jews were stripped of their economic assets and left dependent on some remnants of capital or on charity from overseas. As far as many Germans were concerned, their Jewish neighbors had simply disappeared and it was unsafe to inquire about them. The few Jews who did manage to live out the war in Germany did so by becoming invisible. The terms used for them was U-boats, submarines, who are never seen.

This process of denationalizing and dehumanizing has left a thick layer of suspicion between the Jews and the *goyim*, the strangers. No matter how assimilated, no matter how wealthy or influential the individual Jew might seem, the stranger, all strangers, could suddenly turn on one individual Jew or an entire group of Jews, strip them of their rights and property, and destroy them. This left many Jews reacting with suspicion to strangers, German or not.[2] Such reactions of suspicion are consistent with the findings of psychiatrists studying posttraumatic stress victims. Posttraumatic stress may affect victims of crime, rape, war, or natural disasters. It does not affect everyone under stress but it does affect many. Posttraumatic stress symptoms can be carried over to the next generation, to the children of victims who have had no direct contact with the original stress situation but who identify with the victims.[3] This suspicion of strangers, and especially Germans, has, by this process, affected many Jews all over the world. In turn, events such as the opening of the Holocaust Museum in Washington, D.C., and the publicity surrounding it reenforce the problems of the Jews in Germany who must interface with Germans every day.

Between 1938 and 1941 the Nazis turned from denationalization and dehumanization of individual Jews to the destruction of the physical and cultural structure of Judaism. On the night of November 10, 1938, almost all Jewish institutions and synagogues in Germany and Austria were turned into rubble and broken glass. This was the notorious *Kristallnacht*, the night of broken glass.

In 1939 it was the turn of the Jews of Czechoslovakia and Poland to feel the weight of Nazi terror, now fully developed and bureaucratized.[4]

At the same time, the deportations of the highly assimilated Jews of Holland, France, and Belgium to the Polish ghettos began. These Eastern European ghettos had a different cultural base from that of the Jewish culture of Western Europe. The Western European Jews were totally bewildered by the environment of these Yiddish-speaking settlements and had difficulty in adjusting to these fellow Jews.

From that time on it became impossible for any Jew, anywhere, to think that he or she was exempt from discrimination, to believe that somehow a distinction would be made between his own kind of Jew and the other Jew who differed from him in dress or behavior. All Jews could be forced to become ghetto dwellers once more, without warning.

In 1940 and 1941 the old Jewish communities in the Baltics and the Balkans, as well as those in western Russia, were destroyed; most of their population was killed by the execution squads. These execution squads were composed of Germans and Austrians, but they also contained soldiers drawn from the population of Lithuania, Latvia, and the Ukraine. This was to be remembered by the survivors in post-World War II and would influence the politics of the area.

With the destruction of these communities, the reservoirs of Jewish population, culture, and Jewish learning that had fed the Western European Jewish communities for hundreds of years were eliminated. Except for the Jewish communities of Britain and the United States, there were no major reservoirs of Jewishness (*Yiddishkeit*) from which the survivors of Nazi terror could draw support. Israel, or Palestine as it was called at that time, was considered too marginal and lacking a guarantee of permanence to furnish that cultural and physical support.

The *Sephardic* communities of the Near East and North Africa were too removed culturally from the German or *Ashkenaz* traditions to be considered a reservoir for Jewish rebuilding in Europe. Even some of the *Sephardic* communities in Europe, such as the large Jewish community in Salonika, Greece, died in the Nazi terror.

In 1942 came the "Final Solution," the Nazi attempt to erase every Jew in Europe from the face of the earth. The *Einsatzkommandos*, the special mission units, shot the inhabitants of the ghettos by the thousands, without regard for age or sex. Ghetto after ghetto was liquidated, "cleansed" in the official Nazi terminology. The Nazi labor and extermination camps were designed to kill all the Jews who had escaped the first rain of bullets. Those who lived through this period—whether in exile, in the camps, or in hiding— have become a special group of Jews, the Holocaust survivors. The dictionary defines survivors as "those who lived through changed circumstances or misfortune." It is certainly a useful description for our purposes.

Holocaust survivors have learned through bitter experience not to trust outside organizations, strangers, or even other members of their own group. There are many records of Jews who broke under *Gestapo* pressure and became Nazi informers or hunters of Jews in hiding. Stella, whose biography was published recently, is only one example of a Jewish hunter of Jews.[5] There were Jews who became members of the Jewish ghetto police or the *Judenrat*, the supervising council of a ghetto, one of whose functions was to select Jews for deportation to the death camps.[6] There were other Jews who became *kapos*, concentration-camp group supervisors, some of whom mistreated their fellow prisoners as badly as did the Nazi guards. The knowledge and existence of these Jews who persecuted fellow Jews has an influence on the attitudes and actions of the Jews in Germany today. It is known to almost everyone that most people can be broken if sufficient pressure is applied or that they can be morally undermined in a series of small stages by promises of good treatment for themselves or their families or threats of punishment.[7] This knowledge undermines the establishment of mutual trust.

In the United States and some other countries, Holocaust survivors as well as their children and grandchildren have been accorded a special status of respect in the Jewish communities. This does not seem to be the case among the Jews in Germany. Perhaps this is because so many Jews in Germany are survivors of government persecution, terrorism, or war. There is no classification of the degree of horrors survived by those who went through the Holocaust or the *Gulags*.

One effect on the survivors of persecution is as valid for the Jews in Germany as it is for any other survivors of disaster. Family structures are shattered and are very difficult to restore. Those who have survived may be a mere fragment of a wide circle of friends and relatives who did not survive. Fritz complains that out of his extended family of 200 persons, only six have survived.[8] The children of survivors are thus deprived of acquaintance and relationships with an extended family group and a wide circle of their parents' friends. They lack grandparents, aunts, uncles, and cousins in large numbers—relatives who either died or were never born. It is perhaps this situation that makes loneliness endemic among survivors and their families.

The Third Reich had almost as traumatic an effect on the Germans as it did on the Jews.[9] World War II turned many German cities into brick dust and killed off, either physically or emotionally, much of a generation. The Germans who lived through the war, like many Jews, are afraid to trust in the permanence of anything good.

The Germans have lost their status as an accepted member of those countries distinguished by their joint Western European cultural heritage. The equation: "Germany equals Auschwitz" faces them in intercourse with foreigners of all countries formerly occupied by German troops as well as with all Jews. What one filmmaker calls the "Moment of Silence"[10] is experienced almost universally whenever a Jew meets a German. It is the noticeable moment when conversation stops while both sides make a psychological adjustment. When dealing with individual Jews, the German must face the question: "What did you or your parents do or not do during the Hitler era?" The same question sometimes arises when Germans visit Norway, Yugoslavia, France, or England. It may not be spoken aloud, but it is there nonetheless.[11]

The Germans, too, suffer from broken extended relationships. In their families, too, the young men died at the battlefront, and civilians lost their lives and possessions in the fire storms that consumed cities such as Dresden and Hamburg. They also faced the rape, starvation, and dislocation that occurred as Allied armies occupied Germany in 1945.[12] Many Germans also became refugees as they fled from the advancing Russian armies to the West.[13]

An indirect result of the Nazi philosophy of conquest was the splitting of Germany into different "Zones of Occupation," where the occupiers imposed their own philosophy on the Germans in their zone. The existence of the DDR was a direct consequence of the decisions taken at the end of the war at the Potsdam Conference in 1945. Now most all of those who settled in the DDR, including the Jews who returned, are in the position described by a young German as "Your homeland has vanished . . . it has performed the Great Country Disappearing Act and merged with the country it has always considered its worst enemy."[14] Being a refugee yourself does not engender a great deal of sympathy to other refugees such as Jews fleeing from Russia or Poland.

To all of these barriers to normal relations must be added a factor of fear on the part of the older Germans. Hitler made the Western Allies synonymous with world Jewry. To many older Germans it was the Jews' enmity toward Germany after 1933 that brought about the economic and social boycotts of Germany by the rest of the world. These measures by the Western world were in turn seized by Hitler's propaganda machine to justify his annexations and war. Some blame the Jewish political influence for the demand by the Western powers for unconditional surrender by Germany, for the Morgenthau Plan, and for the other consequences of these policies. Despite the denials of that supposed Jewish influence, many Germans retain their beliefs.

These barriers exist between Jew and German. They can neither be denied nor rationalized away. They must be dealt with if there is to be any discourse between the two groups. That the methods used to deal with these barriers are not 100 percent effective nor work for all members of either group must also be assumed. The officials of both the German and Jewish communities have made extraordinary efforts to reduce these barriers.

In almost every German city there are memorials to former Jewish institutions, either as plaques marking where former institutions once stood or by naming streets or plazas after Jewish individuals or institutions. This practice has now been extended to the cities of the former East Germany, where the name of a Communist anti-Nazi is sometimes replaced by a "Jewish" name. Memorial services, where German government officials appear on the same platform with Jewish dignitaries, are often held on the date of the *Kristallnacht* or the date when the Jews of that particular town were rounded up for deportation. There are memorials at the sites of concentration camps such as Dachau. The Berlin railway officials were recently convinced by public protests to retain and mark the ramps where the Jews of Berlin were loaded on the cattle cars for transport to Poland. Exhibitions have been widely organized that deal with Jewish cultural figures and the role they played in the history of Germany. Such events allow Jewish and German leadership to share a platform and jointly affirm that these events took place then but are not taking place now. They establish a temporal distance between the Germany of Adolf Hitler and of Helmut Kohl. This distancing, by allowing the participants to relive the traumatic events, seems to be an accepted method to minimize the severity of the effects of posttraumatic stress.[15]

The treatment of the Jews by the Germans was one of the touchstones stipulated by John McCloy, U.S. High Commissioner, for judging the reestablishment of German democracy.[16] Financial reparations for the damage done to German Jews and the return of all property the Nazis seized from Jewish individuals and institutions were part of the laws promulgated at the creation of the West German Federal Republic in 1948. The actual working-out of this process in all its details took until 1952 and involved the government of Israel as well as an international committee that evolved into the Conference for Jewish Material Claims Against Germany.[17] The Jews of Germany, as an organized group, were not given a place at the conference table and were not members of the Conference for Jewish Material Claims at that time.[18] This assumption of power by international Jewry to make decisions for the Jews in Germany has not been forgotten by the *Gemeinden* or by many of the individuals in Germany active in Jewish affairs. We will have more to say on this subject in Chapter Seven.

As part of the reparations offered by the German government was a special sum of money to those German Jews willing to return to live in Germany. German Jews were also offered the return of their German citizenship if they desired it. Some of the German Jewish exiles, especially older ones who had not adjusted well to their exile or those German Jews who had settled per force in uncongenial places like Shanghai or the Dominican Republic, took up the offer to return to Germany on favorable terms.

The East German government offered no reparations, though it did offer resettlement and citizenship to returning refugees. The Communists claimed that they were the victims, not the successors, of Hitler's Germany. This legal stand created enormous political, social, and economic problems forty years later when Germany was unified. The reparations laws formulated in 1952 were now considered to apply to the former East Germany as well as West Germany. However, the long time period between when the property was seized and 1990, when Germany was reunified, left the legal status of much of the real estate confused. Property seized by the Nazis and the DDR was to be returned. Property expropriated by the Soviet army between 1945 and 1948, when the DDR was formally established, is not subject to reparations. The long interval has also made documentation much more difficult, and a whole army of lawyers has sprung up to handle the claims.

Reparation of real estate, stores, and factories at this late date causes considerable dislocation and resentment by contemporary Germans. It means moving some tenants who have been living in these formerly Jewish-owned houses for fifty years or trying to relocate day-care centers and similar users for the benefit of people who knew the property only as memories of their parents or grandparents.[19] Chancellor Kohl has now proposed compensating former owners in cash rather than returning property and imposing a heavy tax on those who insist on getting their real estate back. Payments of reparations for seized property in East Germany is postponed in all cases until at least 1996. In the meantime a business has sprung up where investors are buying up the outstanding claims, especially those for property in the center of cities. Large-scale real-estate operators are purchasing these individual claims in an effort to assemble blocks of property to build modern, large-scale office complexes. In these purchases some money is paid "up front," with the rest of the payment coming when the claim is approved. Since the original claimants are now older or a generation removed from being actual victims, there seems to be less of a feeling of repairing the past than there was in the first round of reparations in the 1950s. It has become more of a business transaction dealing with an inheritance and less of dealing with the loss of the old homestead. No matter how the problems of reparations are finally worked out, there is no question that these payments will represent a drain on German budgets for years to come.

Another form of reparations for past damages is inviting former Jewish residents to visit their old hometowns at government expense. This program was first instituted by the Berlin Senate in 1961 and has since been adopted by numerous villages, towns, and cities in Germany. Such visits help both Jews and Germans bridge the gap of the years. Visitors are also encouraged to go to their old schools and talk to the younger generation about the "Old Days." This can sometimes result in a considerable strain on both sides, not only the students, but visitor and host. In one case that came to our attention, the host and organizer of such a program was remembered by the visitor as precisely the leader of the Nazi girls group that had caused her so much pain. It made the talk to the school class into an ethical dilemma whether to tell the whole truth or edit it in deference to the hosts' present position and outlook.

In some ways reparations programs are of more benefit to the Jews living outside of Germany and to the State of Israel, as beneficiaries of deceased Jews without heirs, than they are to the Jews in Germany. Relatively fewer benefits accrue to the *Gemeinden* and to the Jews who have returned to Germany. Much of the property in East Germany is in poor physical condition and will require a great deal of capital to repair and maintain. Another reason for the success of large investors in buying up claims is that these investors have the resources to develop the properties.

A number of other measures taken by the German government are of immediate and direct benefit to the Jews in Germany. Not only does the government collect the membership dues for the *Gemeinde*, but there are also German subsidies to Jewish institutions. Many of the social services, such as the language classes for Russian immigrants, receive government money. Practically the entire cost for the new Jewish museum in Berlin is scheduled to come out of the cultural affairs budget of the City of Berlin. Various local communities pay for the upkeep of the cemeteries or old synagogue buildings in places where there is no active Jewish congregation; such costs are subsidized if the congregation is financially too weak. Jewish representatives sit as equals with Catholics and Protestants on religious boards, despite the fact that Jews only constitute a small fraction of the German population. The same courtesy is not usually extended to the Muslim population, although it is much larger in number, on the grounds that most of the Muslims are only residents, not citizens, of Germany.

Of even greater concern to the Jews of Germany than representation on religious boards is the existence and administration of the laws of asylum. Until July 1993, anyone claiming to be persecuted for national, ethnic, or religious reasons could enter Germany, make an application for asylum, and be eligible for welfare assistance. It would often be years until a case was actually heard and, if rejected, an order for deportation issued. Under this law of asylum, many of the Russian Jews entered the country and are now living on old-age or welfare payments. It is still possible to enter Germany over the "green border"—that is, illegally—since the border guards are not allowed to shoot. Illegal immigrants are not eligible for unemployment or welfare payments and are officially prohibited from working. "Black," or illegal, job opportunities always exist, but the jobs are usually poorly paid, and if one is caught, the illegal worker is immediately deported. Restricting the asylum law causes fear among the Jews that the German government is willing to make concessions to quiet right-wing xenophobia. The majority of the Jews feel that Germany, because of its Nazi history, owes greater consideration to victims of persecution than do other countries. That refugees from Russia, even if in Germany legally, cannot easily become German citizens also concerns those Jews who remember the expulsion of Polish Jews from Germany in 1938 "because they were foreigners."

The recent revival of the political right-wingers, under whatever label, also opens old wounds and revives old fears. Even before the upsurge of overt intolerance in 1992, Jewish institutions were guarded by machine-gun-toting German policemen on the watch against terrorists of all kinds. Armed guards, however, cannot prevent hate phone calls or hate mail, nor can they protect all Jews travelling on public transportation or sitting in taverns from roving gangs of hoodlums shouting Nazi slogans. It does not take a large number of these gangs or many attacks to arouse this fear. The failure of some judges to impose jail sentences for such violence has not reassured the Jews either.

The first German reaction to this new attack on Jews, foreigners, and homosexuals was one of shock. When it became clear that these were not isolated instances of violence but evidence of new right-wing activity that had support even among some of the police and military, the reaction of the majority of the German population was very strong. Thousands and tens of thousands of Germans took to the streets to protest the outrages. The Jewish leadership and some non-*Gemeinde* Jews joined in the candlelight parades to show that 1992 was not 1932. The skin-heads were not deterred by candlelight parades. They were joined in their violence by their opponents, the *Anonyms*, a group of far-left extremists. The battles between these two groups of extremists raised the specter of the beginnings of the Nazi period when private armies of Nazis and Communists dominated the streets. In addition, the new right-wingers, in the form of the "Republican Party," won some eight percent of the vote in a number of local elections. The fact that some of the old imperial war flags had replaced the swastika banners and that the violence at present seemed to be more directed against foreigners than Jews was not reassuring to the *Gemeinde* or to other Jews. Many German states have now banned the old imperial flags as well, but new symbols will undoubtedly be found. The old Hitler slogans and the old songs can still be heard at times, sometimes sung or shouted by young hoodlums and at other times sung by drunken old-timers.[20] The general feeling among the Jews in Germany is that they must oppose these neo-Nazis now, for though foreigners are the main targets today, the Jews will be next on the list of victims.

The German government has taken some countermeasures against the violence, banning some right-wing organizations and raiding the headquarters of right-wing rock groups. The German government also sent out speakers and promulgated publicity to reassure the world in general, and the Jewish world in particular, that Nazi ideology is not returning as the expression of Germany. Any politician, local or national, who makes an injudicious or intentional anti-Jewish remark is immediately removed from office and from membership in the mainline parties. The Jewish leaders, from Mr. Bubis on down, have also tried to reassure the world that Nazism shall not rise again. The success of such a program of public relations is problematical.[21]

The "one-packed-suitcase syndrome" and, in many cases, personal experience with persecution has prevented panic from spreading among the Jews in Germany. In their experience a gravestone overturned or a monument sprayed with unpleasant graffiti does not, by itself, mean that the Nazis are returning to power. Everyone admits that if things get too bad, they would flee to Israel or try to get asylum in the United States. Things do not seem that bad yet. If the physical safety of the Jews in Germany is indeed threatened, there would be little hesitancy in abandoning life in Germany. Unlike the 1930s, the roots of the Jews in Germany in the 1990s are not deep. There would not be the sense of betrayal or surprise that characterized the German Jews' mental outlook of the 1930s if such a development came to pass. The German government is well aware that the Jews might abandon Germany if the right-wing sentiment grew too strong; it is doing everything in its power to reassure the Jews of Germany. The government is also aware that an increase in right-wing activity would lead to a world boycott of Germany. The business community, led by large corporations such as Siemens and Mercedes-Benz, has also taken steps to fight the radicals. The companies have subsidized anti-right-wing demonstrations and have threatened any employee engaged in pro-Nazi activity with immediate dismissal. The cost of a Hitler or Stalin to Germany has been well demonstrated. That lesson has been absorbed by a large majority of both Jews and Germans.

Despite this awareness, it is unlikely that the Hitler era can disappear from German consciousness. The monuments and memorials of the Holocaust will continue to be visible in the streets of German cities. The fate of the old concentration camps is more uncertain, since most of them are off the well-travelled roads and were flimsily constructed in the first place. If the fate of the Matthausen camp near Melk, Austria, is an example, there will be a monument to the victims at the site, with the rest of the space being turned into recreational land. A few of the most infamous camps will probably be maintained with the help of private donations. "Against Forgetting," an organization backed primarily by banks and industry, is planning to raise "millions of marks" to supplement the six million dollars pledged by the Bonn Government to restore the Auschwitz camp in Poland.

On the other hand, the candidate for President of Germany of the ruling party, the Christian Democratic Union, has openly stated that Germany should not have a special role in history because of its Hitlerian past. When that statement was attacked by Mr. Bubis, among others, Chancellor Kohl defended his candidate with the remark, "Steffan Heitmann may not be very much concerned with the wide world but he speaks in very direct language what millions are thinking."[22]

On November 23, 1993 Steffan Heitmann withdrew his candidacy for president of Germany under pressure from many groups for his blunt statements. However Chancellor Kohl still defended Heitmann against what he called "personal attacks."

There has been a steady revival of Germany's imperial past as a tool for rebuilding all-German pride. Frederick the Great's remains have been reinterred in Potsdam, and the uniforms of the eighteenth-century Prussian grenadiers can be seen again in reenactments in both Berlin and Potsdam. The imperial buildings of the *Unter den Linden*, the boulevard in central Berlin designed for presenting the power of the old Reich, are being cleaned and restored. The war memorial, the former tomb of the unknown soldier, is being rededicated to all the dead of both world wars, without singling out a particular group of victims or distinguishing the Nazi soldiers from their targets. All German history is being reunified into a single stream, without giving the Third Reich a special emphasis or ignoring it, as has been done in the recent past.

NOTES

1. The intent to destroy a culture rather than the killing itself makes the Holocaust a particularly Jewish historical event, without wishing to minimize the death of the many other members of various religions and nationalities.

2. John J. Sigal and Morton Weinfeld, *Trauma and Rebirth—Intergenerational Effect of the Holocaust* (New York: Praeger, 1989) and Steven A. Luel and Paul Marcus, eds., *Psychoanalytical Reflections on the Holocaust* (New York: KTAV Publishing House, 1984).

3. Ibid.

4. Reinhard Rurup, *Topographie des Terrors* (Berlin: Verlag Willmuth Arenhovel, 1987).

5. Peter Weyden, *Stella* (New York: Simon & Schuster, 1992).

6. It is far outside the scope of this study to discuss the morality of those Jews who chose to join the *Judenrat* or those who functioned as ghetto police.

7. The same phenomenon has been reported in the prisoner of war camps of the Korean and Vietnam conflicts.

8. Peter Sichrovsky, *Strangers in Their Own Land* (New York: Basic Books, 1986).

9. The question of "guilt" is not within the scope of this study.

10. Deborah Lefkowitz, *Moment of Silence* (Cambridge, Mass.: Lefkowitz Films, 1990).

11. Personal observation.

12. Interviews with German refugees in 1946 made it clear that incidents were most common during the advance of the Russian armies. These incidents were not unknown in towns occupied by soldiers of the Western Allies.

13. Dept. of State, *Occupation of Germany: Policy and Progress 1945–1946*. United States of America Publ. 2783, European Series No. 23 (Washington, D.C.: Aug. 1947).

14. Susan Stern and James G. Neuger, *Ten Went West: East German Students Between Three Worlds* (Bonn: Atlantik Brücke, Aug. 1992).

15. P. A. Saigh, ed., *Post Traumatic Stress Disorder* (New York: Pergamon Press, 1992).

16. Quoted in Y. Michael Bodemann, *State and Ethnicity* in "Jüdisches Leben in Deutschland Seit 1945." (Hamburg: Rowolt, 1993).

17. Work on reparations began under the occupation authorities. See General Lucius D. Clay, *Decision in Germany* (Garden City, N.Y.: Doubleday, 1950). The reparations agreement was signed between the Bundesrepublik Germany and the State of Israel in Luxemburg City, 10 Sept. 1952. The role of the Conference on Jewish Material Claims Against Germany is spelled out in Protocols 1 and 2.

18. At present the representatives of the *Zentralrat* of the Jews in Germany are full members of the Conference.

19. For an example, see Katie Hafner, *The House We Lived In*, "New York Times Magazine," 10 Nov. 1991.

20. Such music was heard under the writer's hotel window in Hamburg, summer of 1991.

21. A. M. Rosenthal, (column) in *New York Times*, 24 Nov. 1992.

22. *Berliner Morgenpost*, 3 Oct. 1993.

Chapter Five

The Legacy of Socialism

Socialism in various forms has had a great influence on the mentality of the Jews in Germany. This influence is as important to the German Jews as it is for Jews who came to Germany from the East. The first wave of Socialist theories that influenced Jewish thought came at the end of the nineteenth century. These theories transformed the old ghetto concept—of the rich giving charity to the poor—into a program of social entitlement for all people. German Jewish reformers like Bertha Pappenheim (1859–1936) fought for the civil and economic rights of unmarried mothers and illegitimate children. The issue she raised concerned not only the physical care of these individuals, but their rights as full members of society instead of as social outcasts. As part of her fight she created a day-care center, trained teachers, and was a founder of the *Jüdischer Frauenbund* (the Jewish Women's League) in 1907. A strong anti-Zionist, she fought for feminine rights until the day of her death, which occurred after she had been interrogated by the Gestapo. The program of equal rights for women, kindergartens for the children of working mothers, and health programs paid for by the State, which had been adopted by the Social Democrats in about 1906, attracted the support of many Jews in Germany. Some of these issues, first raised ninety years ago, are still being fought out in Germany today. Many of the younger Jews are being attracted to the left-of-center political parties because of their support for these issues.

Socialist ideas in various forms became socially acceptable or even popular among the Jewish intelligentsia, particularly after the blood bath of World War I and the terrible social disruptions of the inflation in Germany in 1919–1923. The most brilliant artists, the most popular writers, and the café society in general claimed to be Socialists of a variety of shades. To a large extent this popularity has continued to the present day. It allows an optimism about the possibility of solutions being found to the visible problems of the cities, solutions that are not being offered by capitalist societies. Whether Socialistic ideas actually work is not the issue; it is the hope of solutions that is attractive.

A second wave of Socialistic ideas that influenced all of the world's Jewry was associated with the ideals and theories of modern Zionism. Theodor Herzl, the founder of the movement, adopted many of his social and economic theories of his associate, the economist Franz Oppenheimer (1864–1943).[1] Oppenheimer believed that ownership of land is a basic need of any society and also believed in the communal settlements which were to be formed to work the land. The *Kibbutz* as a method to achieve the settlement of Palestine and the establishment of Israel as a Jewish homeland, for the most part, followed these concepts. Among the modern Zionists there was a strong emphasis on the dignity of agricultural labor, communal ownership of most property and rotating leadership of the *kibbutz*. This is pure socialism. The working out of these ideals in the reality of today's Israel has not always matched the socialistic basic concepts as formulated by Oppenheimer. Today some of the surviving *kibbutz* have established factories on their land and no longer rely solely on agriculture for their cash income.

This is true even of the left-wing *kibbutz* formed by members of the *Mapam* party.[2]

Some of the children raised in the communal pattern of the *kibbutzim* also did not remain in the settlements but are now part of the wave of Israelis living in Germany and enjoying the fruits of capitalism.

Under the spell of Zionism's original ideals, groups of young, nonreligious German Jews joined the organization of the *Blau-Weiss* (Blue-White). In imitation of the German *Wandervögel* (the migratory birds), these young Jews hiked through the countryside. But they sang Hebrew songs instead of German songs and celebrated the Jewish festivals under the open sky. The *Wandervögel* and youth hostelling, as well as the singing of folk songs, were part of a general German romantic movement, some of which was later misused to spread the pseudomythology of Nazi Teutonic Germanism.

The *Blau-Weiss* only lasted from 1919 to 1929, but its influence remained strong among the German Jewish leadership for many years.[3]

The later efforts of the German Jewish community to retrain young Jews for agricultural labor in Palestine had little of the Socialism or optimism of the *Blau-Weiss*; it was an act of desperation to escape the ever-increasing Nazi persecution. The *Hachscharah*, the training for communal living of the 1930s, was a necessity forced by circumstances, not a conscious choice of Socialistic living. Today, many ideals of the *Blau-Weiss* have been resurrected as part of the modern ecological movement.

The Zionist emphasis on the purchase of land introduced the blue and white charity boxes of the Jewish National Fund into most German Jewish homes. The money collected went to buy land for the Jewish settlements in Palestine. Many German Jews who otherwise did not identify themselves with Jewish causes also gave money on festive occasions such as birthdays or anniversaries to plant trees in Palestine. Most had no intention of ever going to Palestine, but they used this means to identify themselves with Judaism, whether they were regular worshippers at a synagogue or not.

Reclaiming the land, the dignity of agricultural labor, and equality between men and women were ideals shared by the Zionists and Lenin's Russia. This similarity of ideals allowed the Soviets to create and advertise a Jewish "homeland" in Russia, the Jewish Autonomous Republic of Birobidjian established in 1928. This settlement outlived both Hitler and Stalin, but Birobidjian never attracted more than 30,000 settlers and never received widespread Jewish support.[4]

Developing the body as well as the mind was also an ideal sponsored originally by the Socialists. In Jewish circles this idea was taken up by the *Maccabi* athletic clubs. The *Gemeinden* of many cities did not oppose this new emphasis on athletic prowess. Until 1938, the Berlin *Gemeinde* maintained its own athletic stadium. In the 1936 Olympics, much to Hitler's dismay, three Jewish women swept the fencing championships. The athletic movement as symbolized by the *Maccabi* movement, with both Jewish boys and girls with their heads uncovered and dressed only in shorts and blouses, did not fit in with the ideals and beliefs of the Orthodox Jewish community. The pictures of Jewish youths engaged in sports rather than studying the *Talmud* helped to create the image among many of the Orthodox that German Jews were not real Jews. This image persists among some of them to the present day.

Physical development and experience in communal living, as practiced by Socialistically inclined Jews, turned out to have high survival value during the years of the Holocaust. Muscular Jewish youths were more likely to be chosen for work in the Nazi labor camps and managed to survive, at least for a while. Their pale, narrow-chested scholarly brethren were more likely to be marched directly to their deaths by the concentration camp guards, together with the young children and elderly people not suited for hard physical labor. Tuberculosis, typhoid, and other diseases of the ghettos and camps were also more likely to be fatal to those with weaker bodies. Thus, survivors of the Holocaust both in Germany and in Eastern countries are more often found to be members of the *Maccabi* or Zionist groups than graduates of the Jewish religious seminaries. This differentiation in the likelihood of survival is equally true for those who lived in hiding, survived the camps, or fought with the partisans in the forests of Poland and Russia. The disproportion in the Holocaust survivors between athletes and scholars has left an imprint on the present population of the Jews in Germany.

The many members of the political Left, who were the parents or members of the present Jews in Germany, have given this community a strong working-class heritage. Many of the Eastern European Jews who emigrated to Germany in the period between 1906 and 1920 were members of the *Bund*, the General Jewish Workers Association. As workers and self-employed artisans, they brought the program and the organization of the *Bund* with them to Germany. Lenin and other Communist leaders argued that there was no need for a separate Jewish workers group, but the *Bund* and most of the membership persisted with their separate Yiddish emphasis on Socialism. Partly as a result of this struggle for independence, the *Bund* joined the Socialist wing rather than the Communist wing of the Marxists. The *Bund* was not Zionist in orientation,[5] concentrating instead on economic issues. It was only in the 1950s that those Socialists interested in Zionism organized the *Pa'oli Zion*, a political party that later became part of the *Mapai* party in Israel. The nationalist Zionists or *Revisionists* who believed in taking Palestine as a Jewish homeland by force of arms congregated in the *Betar*. Despite their emphasis on military preparedness, the nationalists, too, believed in establishing Socialist-type *kibbutzim*.

Most of the Orthodox groupings damned Zionism and Socialism alike until after World War II. Joseph Schneerson, the predecessor of the present head of the *Lubavitcher Hasidim*, suggested that it might be better for the Jews to die under the Nazis in Europe than to lose both body and soul under the godless Zionist.[6] This was, of course, before the full horror of the Holocaust was known. Some of the Orthodox Jews, such as the *Satmar Hasidim*, still do not recognize the State of Israel as a fulfillment of the Jewish dream of a return to the Holy Land. They simply consider Israel a secular state like any other secular government. These viewpoints have left the socialistically inclined Zionists in a much stronger political position among the Jews in Germany than are the Orthodox religious groups. As indicated in other chapters of this study, the existence of the State of Israel is of considerable importance in the self-identification of the Jews in Germany, even among those who have no intention of ever going there to live.

Rosa Luxemburg and Karl Radeck exemplify a still more radical left-wing Jewish tradition than that of the *Bund*. This is the tradition of Communism and anarchism that still play a role in present-day Germany. Rosa Luxemburg, of Polish birth, was primarily active in Germany. She is still a very strong role model among all left-wingers in Germany, not just among the Jews. She and Karl Liebknecht broke with the Social Democrats over the issue of financing the German war effort in World War I, claiming that the workers of the world should unite rather than fight for their various "Fatherlands." She was a leader in the German *Spartakist* uprisings in 1918 and pushed for her own program of feminism and general strikes, even against the opposition of Lenin himself. She was murdered by right-wing militarists in 1919. Because of her early and violent death, she is a more popular figure today than is Karl Radeck, another German Jewish Communist. Radeck went along with Lenin's policies and worked in Moscow as well as in Germany. He was eliminated in the Stalinist purges of the 1930s.

Besides their political program the Communists offered an additional advantage to some of the Jews in Germany. Officially, and to a great extent in reality, the Communist Party did not discriminate against Jews nor put them into a special division. Religion, of course, was frowned upon, but Jewish origin or cultural heritage was no drawback to advancement.

Despite the splintering of the German Communists into Stalinist and Trotskyist wings, despite the purges and betrayals within the Communist Party, many German Communists remained faithful to their ideals. The German Jewish Marxists who returned from exile after World War II, to help rebuild the peaceful and democratic

Germany of their dreams, went to the DDR rather than to West Germany. Many of them rose to prominence in the postwar era, although they all came under suspicion in the period of Stalin's anti-Jewish campaign of 1952. Albert Norden, of the old German Communist Party, returned from New York to become a member of the Central Committee of the Socialist Unity Party of East Germany. The Eisler brothers, one a composer and the other a writer, returned from the United States to become active in East German cultural affairs. Hilda Benjamin became East Germany's Minister of Justice. John Heartfield, the originator of photomontage, went to the DDR to pick up his career from where he had left off in 1933. Bertold Brecht and his Jewish wife built up a repertory theater in East Berlin. These are just some of the more famous of the many Jews who shared Marxist ideas and went back to the DDR from New York, Moscow, or Shanghai.

The DDR died of economic depression and shame in 1990, but many of the Marxists and their children are still fighting actively for their Socialist-oriented program. As the present German government cuts social programs, wages, and funds for abortion in the name of economic competitiveness, an opposition party, the Party for Democratic Socialism (PDS), attracts some of the younger Jews. The two leaders of this party, Gregor Gysi and Andre Brie, are both half-Jews. Their slogans fit into the Jewish ethics. Gysi often repeats a slogan from the *Communist Manifesto*: "When the individual is free, all are free."[7] The policy of a free German society without nationalism and imperialism attracts many Jews, though the PDS as a party organization is not necessarily trusted. Many Jews are attracted to the left-wing parties because they have difficulty allying themselves with the present ruling party whose official title is "Christian Democratic Union" and has close ties with the Catholic hierarchy.

The fact that the Communists' anti-Semitic activities forced most of the Jewish functionaries to flee from the East to the West in 1952 is explained today as the mistake of Stalin, not as a policy of the Communists in general. The anti-Israel stand of the DDR is not always scorned, even by Jews. Socialism, in theory, though not as practiced in the discredited DDR, is still attractive to many Jews in Germany today.

The lack of a firm program by the ecologically minded Green Party and the newly formed Non-Party makes their attractiveness to Jews in Germany difficult to evaluate.

The shock of the government's collapse in the Soviet Union as well as in the DDR has left many of the ideologically oriented Marxists personally and psychologically adrift. Many Jews who had an active role in the DDR have lost their jobs and social position. Some of them are accused of spying on their friends and associates for the East German secret police, the *Stasi*. The revelations of official corruption, favoritism, and the massive ecological damage revealed as part of the DDR's basic structure has undermined trust in Socialist solutions to today's problems. There is, however, a massive readjustment required from a society that provided care from the cradle to the grave for most to a *laissez-faire* capitalism where competitiveness becomes of prime importance and "the devil takes the hindmost."

The Jews in Germany who had shared in the Socialist world of East Germany reacted in a variety of ways. Some continued to battle for government-subsidized social services, thus justifying their lifelong convictions. Some engaged in a romanticism of the DDR, telling tales of the "good old days." Others joined in the capitalist scramble, speculating in real estate and currencies. In this they are joined by Jews from West Germany. It is interesting to note, however, that even the wildest speculators have retained a sense of social responsibility dictated by Jewish ethics. Multi-million-dollar donations have been made by these speculators to causes like Jewish education, general health problems, and cultural activities, both in Germany and in Eastern countries. Some of these donations have been announced with great fanfare, but many were given quietly or even anonymously. This new pattern of giving is closer to the ethics of the ghetto than to Socialism, which advocated taxing the rich to support the poor in a manner to be determined by the State.

The old Socialistic ideas are not dead in the Jewish community. As the German government limits support for immigrants and welfare for troubled families, the Jewish *Gemeinde* will be called upon to fill the gap. If that takes place, the *parnasse* (the wealthy Jews) will be called upon by social pressure to pay for the poor. The situation at present and probably for the next few years is too unstable to predict how the struggle of Socialist and ghetto ethics will work out among the Jews in Germany.

NOTES

1. For a summary of the history of early Zionism and the ideas of Franz Oppenheimer, see *Encyclopedia Judaica* (New York: Macmillan, 1972).

2. Kibbutz Ein Dor, in Galilee, was founded in 1949 by members of the left-wing *Hashomer Hatzair*. Today its main income is derived from a factory that produces coated electric cable. Alisa Barkan, *Personal Communication*.

3. Interviews with Lucie Suhl, a *Blau-Weiss* group leader in Kassel and Leipzig in the years 1919–1921.

4. Martin Gilbert, *A Jewish Historical Atlas* (New York: William Morrow, 1993).

5. The World Conference of the *Bund* in New York in 1949 stated: "The Jewish people are and will remain a people of the world, nine-tenths of them living outside Palestine." (New York: YIVO archives).

6. Quoted in Jonathan Mark, *Broadway Orchestras Fiddled While Ghetto Burned*, in "Jewish Week," 16 Apr. 1993.

7. Among other occasions, at a New York seminar on 4 Apr. 1993.

Chapter Six

Jews and Germans

In June 1990 the *Spiegel*, an influential German weekly news magazine, published an article entitled "Germany only with Jews." In it Lothar de Maziere, an influential East German politician is quoted: "Germany without Jews never existed. Germany only exists with its Jews or it will disappear."[1] Lothar de Maziere was the last prime minister of East Germany, and his statement was a complete reversal of German governmental policy of fifty years earlier. At that time all German publications quoted governmental leaders in demanding a Germany free of Jews, *Judenrein*. Both of these policies were announced within one lifetime. The relatively sudden and violent political and social reversals in the status of Jews in Germany have left both Germans and Jews ambivalent, feeling guilty and angry in their personal and official intercourse.

Just how explosive this issue can still be is illustrated in the small Bavarian city of Passau. In 1981 a sixteen-year-old student, Anna Elizabeth Rosmus, published an essay on everyday life in the Third Reich. In it she mercilessly exposed the evasions and actions of the town's citizens during the Hitler era, naming names and giving details. Her story was the basis of the Oscar-winning film, "The Nasty Girl," in 1990. The film and the events pictured in it tore the town apart. A few citizens backed the printing of these exposures; the majority condemned them. As a local citizen told the author in 1990: "She used her hostility to attack what are now decent citizens for acts they may have committed as young teen-agers." Others have sued Anna Rosmus for libel. Her latest book, "Wintergreen,"[2] has a foreword by Ignatz Bubis and deals with the forced abortions and deliberate fatal neglect of the children of slave laborers near Passau. Ignatz Bubis writes in his foreword that this book belongs in every German school. Mrs. Rosmus has refused to obey the libel rulings of the German courts and is now a student at Boston University, working on a thesis of the history of the Jews in Passau.

The German right wing has been willing to take up the challenge. Several thousand of them planned to hold their convention in Passau in October 1993. The battle lines are drawn once again about the events of fifty years ago, and today's citizens of Passau, as elsewhere, cannot stand aside.

Not all of these problems can be attributed to Hitler and his cohorts. Some of them are deeply rooted in German history and German law. The slogan, "The Jews are our misfortune," was not coined by the Nazis, but by the respected German historian Heinrich von Treitschke in the year 1879. It was about the same time that all Jews were expelled from the German student fraternities of all universities as "non-Germans." In 1883 there were anti-Semitic riots in Stettin (Prussia) and elsewhere. They were stirred up, in part, by the court chaplain of Emperor Wilhelm II, the Reverend Adolf Stoecker. Manifestations of official anti-Semitism can be found at other times as well. In 1916 the German War Ministry undertook a census to determine whether an adequate number of Jews had volunteered for military service. Since they found that a very high percentage of Jews had volunteered—contrary to their expectations—the results of that census were not published until after the war.

The blame for the defeat of Germany and the event that actually forced the end of the war, the revolt of the German High Seas fleet in Kiel in 1918 was blamed on Jewish Communist leaders such as Rosa Luxemburg, Trotsky (Bronstein), and Kautzky. The Communists have always taken credit for that revolt, a claim that furnished fodder to Hitler's propaganda. In some German nationalist circles, the Jews were also blamed for exploiting German inflation of 1919–1923 by buying up German assets cheaply with foreign currencies. There were of course many voices defending the Jews, but the very fact that the Jews needed defenders showed the dangerous potential of this issue.[3]

Refugees from Poland and Russia were especially unpopular with the Germans. Police raided the *Scheunenviertel* repeatedly in 1920 and 1923, looking for illegal aliens. That section was also characterized in the press as an area for prostitution and fencing stolen goods. This was, of course, an era when the disturbed social and economic situation made both prostitution and currency speculation endemic, as the art and literature produced at that time shows. However, the Jews of the *Scheunenviertel* were singled out as the greatest evil doers. Even the German Jews kept themselves apart from these black-dressed figures with beards and side locks who had come from the ghettos of Eastern Europe. On 5 April 1933, the police and Nazi SS staged a raid on this section of Berlin. The pictures taken that day were printed repeatedly in German newspapers and magazines to show how "un-German" the Jews really were.[4]

On the other hand, it has been found difficult to write a history of German culture, business, or science of the nineteenth and twentieth centuries without including the contributions of German Jews. Hitler and his propaganda minister, Joseph Goebbels, attempted to write such a history without Jews. This meant they had to eliminate the lyric poetry of Heinrich Heine, the music of Felix Mendelssohn, the impressionistic paintings of Max Lieberman, the medical research of Paul Ehrlich, the business activities of Joseph Rathenau in founding the electric companies, as well as all the publishing ventures of the Mosse and Ullstein families. There were a similar number of large, gaping holes in the story of German film and theater. The problem of rewriting history was made worse for the Nazis by the fact that Goebbels also proscribed the works of all non-Jewish opponents of the Nazis. Thus, the novels of Thomas Mann, the children's stories of the popular author Erich Kastner, all the works of the German expressionist painters, the designs of the *Bauhaus*, and the pacifist posters of Kaethe Kollwitz joined the works of the Jews in the bonfires lit by the "cultural cleansing" of the Nazis.

All these works, prohibited in Germany between 1933 and 1945, have now been reintroduced into German textbooks as representing the best in German culture, to the confusion of German students. Reintroduction of the work of such Jews who lived and died in Germany has been relatively easy to do. Only a line or even a word is added to show that this artist, scientist, musician, or businessman was Jewish. It is much harder to introduce the work of Jewish intellectuals who left Germany and stayed in exile or of those who died in the concentration camps. In such cases, the schoolbooks or business histories have to include a more complete explanation of what happened to these people after 1933 and so keep the story of the Nazis alive. The problem also exists in the small towns and villages that wish to publish local histories. The situation in the town of Passau has been already described. The town of Dachau, formerly an artist colony and now a pleasant suburb of Munich is another town with an image problem.

The Jewish authors, scientists, and artists who survived the Nazi period by living in other countries after fleeing Germany may also feel a personal ambivalence in their identity. Under what nationality should they allow themselves to be listed? Are they Germans, German Jews, Americans, or what?

This same confusion of self-identity also affects some Jews who fought against Germany in the ranks of the Allies in World War II. If they still consider themselves German, might they not be considered traitors by other Germans? The accusation has certainly been made on occasion.[5] The problem of identity is even worse for those who, like Henry Kissinger, later U.S. Secretary of State, served as military government administrators of Germany during the Allied occupation after World War II. What kind of individuals were they in that position? Legally, of course, they were Allied soldiers. However, sometimes they acted as Germans who were ridding their country of an evil government. At other times they used their special knowledge of German and Germany in the service of their new homeland. On still other occasions they might be primarily acting as Jews, helping the flow of illegal immigrants from Poland into Germany or aiding the emigration of Jews, again illegally, to Palestine. Now they are often asked by the agencies of today's German government to return and visit their "homeland."

The psychological strain of finding an acceptable identity is considerable, both on the German Jews and on the Germans who come into contact with them. This psychological pressure has been continued over the years by, among other things, the reparations paid to those German citizens of Jewish heritage now living in other countries as well as those living in Germany. The problems of accepting what has sometimes been called "blood money" and the revival of the bitter memories came up for the recipients of West German reparations in 1952 and now again with potential payments made from East Germany. To substantiate such claims it is often necessary to dredge up old documents and photographs and solicit corroborating statements from friends and relatives.

The laws that regulate just who is a German citizen also lead to a blurring of identity of the Jews in Germany. Under the basic German law—in force in 1993 but based on much earlier regulations—all people of German origin and culture, no matter when or to what country their ancestors emigrated from Germany, are entitled to reclaim German citizenship and the right of residency in Germany. Under this law, the Volga Germans, whose forefathers emigrated to Russia in the eighteenth century, can and do claim the right to return to Germany now. Presumably, the "Pennsylvania Dutch" would also be so entitled if they desired it. Interim citizenship in another country is no barrier. Therefore, all German Jews, their children, grandchildren, and great-grandchildren are also entitled to this privilege. Baltic, Polish, and Russian Jews, even if their families always spoke German and resided in Germany prior to 1933, or even if they were born in Germany, are not entitled to citizen status.[6] They can only enter Germany as asylum-seekers or visitors. Germany today maintains the legal fiction that all its citizens are of "German blood" on which their citizenship is based. All others are simply residents of Germany subject to travel and other restrictions and even possible deportation in the future.

In reality, as opposed to the legal fiction, at least two groups of German citizens do not fit into this concept of German blood and German culture. One group is the *Sorbs*, living in the *Spreewald* region near Berlin. This group is culturally and linguistically Slavic, not Germanic. The second group is the German Jews who also do not fit into the classification of "German blood," although some writers now and in the past have tried to make them so. In fact, these two groups are minorities whose very existence forms the thin wedge for the idea that there is a multicultural Germany, not a state united by "German blood." As refugees from many other countries have flooded into Germany, there has been much discussion of multiculturalism, but the posters demanding tolerance and rights for the refugees still call them *Ausländer* (foreigners). Until now the German governments, both East and West, have issued postage stamps celebrating the culture of both the German Jews and the *Sorbs*. No such stamps have been issued yet honoring the culture of other minorities whose numbers may be greater than either Jews or *Sorbs*. The Gypsies, or Romanies, who have resided in Germany since the 1400s come to mind.

As citizens, German Jews sit on government commissions, run for election to public office, and are officially treated as equal to the Protestant and Catholic religious bodies. But the Jews in Germany, as German Jews, have also demanded and obtained special privileges as victims of Nazism not accorded to other Germans, victims or not. The reparations of property from the DDR is to be taxed at a lower rate for Jews than the property returned to Germans that had been confiscated either by the Nazis or the East German government. The justification given for this preferential treatment is that Jewish property was seized simply because its owner was a Jew, not for any acts on the part of the individual. Jews, because they are Jews, can refuse to serve in the German armed services because of its association with the old *Reichswehr*, the German army under whose auspices most of the crimes of the Holocaust were committed. Such special treatment has caused considerable resentment on the part of some Germans, particularly those born after World War II. It is difficult for many citizens of the old DDR to see why they, already disadvantaged compared to their West German cousins, should now give up their land or their homes because that land or those houses had been wrongfully seized by a German government more than fifty years ago. What is more, some citizens are expected to give their land to Jews who are not even living in Germany and do not plan to return. They simply wish to sell the real estate at a profit. They resent what they feel to be an injustice and sometimes take out their anger on refugee Jews from the East who have fled to Germany. This is easier than finding a West German or foreign Jew to attack.

The German citizenship laws have also created two classes of Jews within the Jewish community itself. Some of the Jews in Germany are classed as German citizens while others are classed as foreigners. Yet all Jews must be treated as equals by the *Gemeinden*, which is a quasi-governmental agency designed to represent German Jews.

With all this ambivalence, it is extremely difficult for either the Jewish community or many of the individual Jews in Germany to achieve a firmly delineated identity. Depending on the setting or the circumstances, they can be Germans or foreigners, valued members of the German society, hated aliens, or as one group of Jewish writers called it, "Strangers in their own Land."[7]

Chancellor Kohl has recently suggested legislation that might alleviate some of these ambivalences, but only for the next generation. He has proposed that children born in Germany and having gone to German schools for at least nine years be entitled to claim German citizenship, if they wish, upon reaching eighteen years of age. Residents who have lived in Germany and can show fluency in the German language would also be able to apply for citizenship. Though this legislation is being introduced for the benefit of the multimillion-strong Turkish minority, it would help many Jews as well.

The German population is also confused about what status they should accord the Jews in Germany. Perhaps one reason for their uncertainty in establishing personal relationships with individual Jews is their fear of rejection because of the horrors committed on the Jews in the name of the German nation. At the same time, there can be a feeling of unease and even fear in the presence of members of this somewhat mysterious and seemingly indestructible minority that receives such powerful support from overseas. Since the Germans can find no appropriate way to see the Jews, it is often easier for them to avoid the subject of Jews altogether.

The fact that so many Germans have, to their knowledge, never met a Jew personally does not prevent them from having these feelings of confusion, guilt, and fear. This is particularly true of more than half the German population that was not yet born when World War II ended. They know the Nazi era only from history books or perhaps from the stories of their parents and grandparents. Yet they are often exhorted publicly to "come to terms with this terrible period of German history." However, to do so leaves them with an extremely uncomfortable formulation: "The Nazis were evil. My parents, grandparents, or community were Nazis or acquiesced in the Nazi actions. Therefore my parents, grandparents, or community are evil."[8] Many Germans, of the older and younger generations, avoid this discomfort either by claiming that they knew nothing about the more extreme facets of the Holocaust or, while honoring the victims of the Nazis as a group, avoid dealing with any specifics. The mind-set of the Jews is easier. To many of the actual victims, the Holocaust represents specific actions carried out by specific individuals. Thus the equation: "Germans are Nazis" is avoided. Those Jews who believe that almost all Germans were Nazis have left the country and are unlikely to return for an extended stay. If they do come, they visit Dachau or Auschwitz but avoid visiting the present Jewish communities whose very existence diminishes the effect of the Holocaust to them. We have met a number of such visitors as well as many other Jews who cannot bring themselves to visit Germany at all.

Nor are all the Nazis dead. A German doctor was nominated as head of the World Medical Association in 1993. When it was revealed that he had been at least a witness, if not an active participant in the Nazi euthenasia program, his candidacy was rejected. Dr. Vilmar, president of the German Chamber of Physicians, blamed the World Jewish Congress for organizing that rejection.[9] Though it was highly emotional, as the Demanjanjuk trial in Israel proved, the issue of punishing former Nazis is diminishing as time passes and these old men die off.

Since the Germans lack knowledge about the Jews among them and Jews have been a major factor in recent German history, there is considerable curiosity by many Germans about Jews and Jewish culture. Exhibitions of Jewish artifacts or history are visited by many more non-Jews than Jews. German Jewish visitors to Germany are often treated as talking artifacts. If they avoid equating all Germans with Nazis, the visitors are even more welcome, since they help give the Germans back some of their self-esteem.[10]

Neither exhibitions of Jewish artifacts nor visits by old German Jews will be sufficient to establish a valid status for the Jews in German society. The failure to fit and be fitted into a convenient identity remains for them as it does for so many other minorities, worldwide. It is unlikely that this situation will change in Germany in the near future.

NOTES

1. *Spiegel*, vol. 20, 1990.
2. Anna Rosmus, *Wintergrün-Verdrängte Morde* (Konstanz: Labhard Publishers, 1993).

3. For a summary of German anti-Semitism before Hitler, see *Juden in Preussen* 2d ed. (Dortmund: Harenberg Kommunication, 1981).

4. Eike Geisel, ed., *Im Scheunenviertel* (Berlin: Severin and Siedler, 1981).

5. Personal observation.

6. For an example of such problems of citizenship, see *Ein Jude Kann Nicht Deutscher Sein*, in "Semitimes," No. 5, 1992.

7. Peter Sichrovsky, ed., *Strangers in Their Own Land* (New York: Basic Books, 1986).

8. There are studies of the psychological difficulties of the children of Nazi leaders, but they are not part of this book.

9. Jennifer Seaning, *German Doctors and Their Secrets*, in *New York Times*, 26 1993.

10. Personal observation.

Chapter Seven

The Jews in Germany and World Jewry

The Jewish population in Germany does not exist in a global vacuum. It is closely tied both politically and emotionally to the Jewish communities elsewhere, especially to the communities in Israel, the United States, and the successor states of the former Soviet Union.

In 1945–1946 the surviving Jews of Central and Eastern Europe lived huddled in the displaced persons camps, the majority of them in the U.S. occupation zone in Western Germany. The residents of these camps were, despite the best efforts of the occupation authorities and such organizations as UNNRA and the Joint Distribution Committee, underfed and underclothed. In addition the camps were severely overcrowded, holding a large number of illegal refugees from Poland together with their listed population of ex-slave laborers and concentration camp inmates. The psychological damage inflicted on these survivors by both the Nazis and the Polish and Lithuanian population was still very raw and the wounds had not yet formed scabs.[1] All the Jews who had survived the Holocaust could not avoid being extremely hostile to any outside authority, a result of the maltreatment by the authorities of camps and ghettos. They had survived by their wits and by evasion of regulations. Now they evaded the regulations of both the newly organized German police and the U.S. Army Constabulary.[2] Internal administration of the D.P. camps was firmly in the hands of the Zionists. Preparations for emigration to Israel were carried on everywhere, whether in the form of *Hachscharah*, the training for kibbutz life, or the teaching of Hebrew.[3] Political pressure was being exerted by the Jews of many countries to force the British government to open Palestine to Jewish immigration, and one of the weapons in that fight was the poor conditions in the Jewish D.P. camps. Those Jews who wished to stay in Germany instead of signing up to go to Israel were considered traitors by many of their fellow Jews and were subjected to sanctions such as removal from jobs within the camps.[4] This attitude was not only expressed by Zionist camp inmates but by many of the American Jewish authorities and administrators as well. Illegal immigration to Palestine was also aided by an informal but effective network of Jewish servicemen in the armies of occupation. Members of my own small Air Force unit helped a trainload of illegal Jewish immigrants from Poland reach the Landsberg D.P. camp by bribing the German train crew with two cartons of cigarettes and by riding with the train to the camp. We also "liberated" captured enemy military materiel for the Jewish Defense Forces in Palestine. Transportation of this materiel was arranged by the Jewish chaplain. Similar activity was reported by members of the Jewish Brigade serving in the British Army.

The official American attitude toward this pressure on Jews to emigrate from Germany was expressed by General Lucius D. Clay, Commander of the U.S. forces in Europe. "It would be a mistake for Jewish leaders to demand that all Jews leave Germany," he wrote. "They should insist on their right to remain and participate in the future of Germany."[5] However, few active steps were taken to implement such a policy prior to the establishment of the German Federal Republic in 1948. The American and British authorities were hard-pressed to find enough Germans free of Nazi affiliations for the major programs of government without devoting manpower to what seemed to them to be peripheral issues.

The official world Jewry stepped up the pressure to create a Germany free of Jews even after the establishment of an independent Germany. Thus, they inadvertently worked to carry out Hitler's wishes and create a Germany free of Jews. At the World Jewish Congress in Frankfurt, Germany, in July 1950, speakers demanded that the Jews in Germany be given no vote since "there were no Zionists left in Germany." A month later the Jewish Agency told all Jews in Germany to pack their bags and be ready to leave within six weeks since the agency was closing its office in Munich. At the October meeting of the World Jewish Congress, a speaker demanded that all contact with the Jews in Germany be broken off.[6] The Jews in Germany were given no role in the negotiations about reparations that lead to the signing of the Treaty of Luxemburg between West Germany, Israel, and the Committee for Jewish Material Claims Against Germany.[7] The policy of treating the Jews in Germany as a community in transit to Israel or in liquidation may have been dictated as much by the need of numerous immigrants to strengthen Israel in its struggle against the onslaught of Arab armies as it was by hostility to Germany. In any case, it seemed to the Jews living in Germany that world Jewry, especially the Zionists, wanted to treat the Jews in Germany as second-class Jews. The attitude that no "real Jews" would visit or live in Germany was expressed to us many times by Jews living in America, before we visited Berlin in 1985. This was as true of American-born Jews as it was of refugees from Europe. It was the attitude of the majority of Jews in Israel and in the United States. Officially, the Jewish attitude was beginning to change in 1956. In Israel that year the *Gemeinde* of the Jews in Germany was admitted as a member to the Zionist Congress. The chairman of the *Zentralrat* was invited to sessions of the Joint Distribution Committee and to the Claims Conference. In 1959 Heinz Galinski of Berlin was elected president of the World Jewish Congress.[8]

The position of the Jews in Germany with regard to their relation with Israel had already improved in 1951, when the government of Israel entered into negotiations with the West German government and established an Israeli mission in Bonn in 1952. Officials and other Israelis began to come to Germany. Obviously, if the State of Israel could negotiate with the German government, the Jews living in Germany could no longer be considered traitors by world Jewry. This, in turn, made it possible for the Jews in Germany to see Israel as not only a place to emigrate, but as a place from which they could draw pride and self-confidence. Articles published about Israel in the *Allgemeine Jüdische Wochenzeitung* rose from 13 percent of all articles in 1950 to 34 percent in 1986.[9] The Jewish papers in Germany began to advertise trips to Israel for German visitors. Israeli teachers were hired by Jewish schools and day-care centers. Israeli kosher food of Middle Eastern origin began to be available in Germany, and Israeli gift stores were found in cities like Hamburg, Berlin, and Frankfurt. More Israelis came to Germany to live and work. The present number of Israelis in Germany is estimated to be near 10,000, a considerable proportion of all the Jews in Germany. Israel has become a place to take pride in for the Jews in Germany, even for the many who have no plans to settle there.

This did not mean that everything was now going smoothly between the Israelis and the Jews in Germany. In July 1982 a number of Jews in Berlin formed the "Jewish Group," now part of the "Democratic List," to protest the Israeli invasion of Lebanon. Criticism of the Israeli policy toward the Arabs has continued among many of the liberal Jews. The coming of peace between the Israelis and the Palestinians, if such a peace actually comes to pass, may cause an alteration in this attitude.

On the other hand, the outspoken Israeli education minister was quoted as saying in December 1992: "I am amazed that there are still Jews living in Germany. It depends of course whether they consider themselves to be Jews or Germans."[10] Israeli government officials have consistently and officially criticized both the Jewish community in Germany and the Bonn government for allowing

Russian Jews to stay in Germany rather than insisting that they continue their trip to Israel.[11]

Israel has always considered itself to be the guardian of all the Jews in the world. The *Yad Vashem*, the memorial of remembrance in Jerusalem, is considered the ultimate authority on all phases of the Holocaust, denying any authority to speak about the Holocaust to the German Jews. Like all guardianships, such a relationship implies inequality, and some of the Jews in Germany resent this assumption of inequality. Michael Wolffsohn argues that Israel was only made possible by the actions of the German Jews.[12] All in all, however, Israel is regarded by most Jews in Germany as a Jewish bastion, and any disagreements between the Israelis and the Zionists are simply arguments within the Jewish family.

The United States, as the major world power, was and is considered to be the political guardian of the Jews in Germany, not only in Jewish circles, but by many Germans as well. Pressure from the United States government helped force through the implementation of the German policy of reparations. It is considered that the American Jews, exerting whatever pressures are necessary on the American government, ensure that the Jews in Germany are not injured by any German revival of anti-Semitism. The outbreak of incidents of Nazi-type violence in Germany in the fall of 1992 was extensively reported by the U.S. press, and the *New York Times* called for an international commission to supervise German government reaction to this violence.[13] Events such as President Reagan's visit to the World War II cemetery at Bitburg, where some SS men are buried, brought an immediate outcry from the American Jewish community. The large Holocaust museum built on federal land in Washington, D.C., is another instance of the American concern for Jewish sensibilities.

Political protection is only part of the major role that America and its Jews play in the life of the Jews in Germany. The number of Jews in Germany who have relatives in the United States is fairly high. What they hear about the life of these relatives in America, despite all disclaimers, still makes it seem like America is the

"Golden Land" of the Jews. Most of the recent immigrants to Germany, or to Israel for that matter, would have preferred to come to America. In America most Jews own their own homes or apartments, and their families have from one to three automobiles. Their children can go to college, and they can enter any profession. Despite an occasional incident like the riot in Crown Heights, New York, there is relatively little overt anti-Semitism in the United States. The fact that the Jews in America are wealthy, so think most Jews in Germany, shown first by the financial support given to the Jews in the D.P. camps. More recently, the Americans have again provided financial support to provide for the refugees from Russia. The Lauder Foundation of New York subsidized the Jewish summer camps in Europe and the *Lubavitchers* draw on American funds to publish their magazine in German and to send their emissaries all over Europe. The misconception of unlimited wealth attributed both to individual American Jews and to the corporate Jewish community can lead to demands for support at all levels. Failure to send this money to Europe is often interpreted as American hard-heartedness and stinginess. Since the unification of Germany, there has been an influx of American capital into Europe, particularly into Berlin and East Germany. Some of this capital comes from firms known to be Jewish-owned and extends the image of the rich Americans even into banking circles in Germany.

This conception of America as the "Golden Land" or, perhaps more accurately, as the "Land of Gold" does not extend to approving the actions taken by Americans or the American government. The war in Vietnam and the military actions taken in Grenada, Panama, and Iraq were criticized severely in some Jewish circles in Germany. But in conversation at least many Jews in Germany wish their children to go to America or at least to learn English.

Relations between the Jews in Germany and the Jewish communities in the former Soviet Union is still in flux. There are still some two million Jews living in those countries. Some would probably like to emigrate to the United States, Israel, or Germany, while others are trying to build up strong Jewish communities in various cities.

There is considerable economic distress in Russia and the Baltic republics. Appeals for help in food, medicine, and ritual Jewish material for these areas are published regularly in the *Jüdische Korrespondenz*. Some of this help is sent, help for rebuilding synagogues and for caring for the Jewish sick and elderly. As in the United States, accounts of Jewish life in Russia often appear in the German press. Fear of sudden political instability, with the potential of sending two million refugees over the German border, is a nightmare of both German and Jewish authorities. The flare-up of fighting in Georgia and along the border of Tadjikstan, as well as the increasing Islamic influence of the Asiatic republics, have already increased the flow of Jewish immigrants from those regions.

It is difficult to appraise the economic and social relationships between the emigré Russian Jewish community and the residents in their old homelands. Large corporate deals occasionally appear in the financial press, but most of the trade involves much smaller sums and amounts of merchandise. Residents travel both ways, sometimes with empty suitcases one way. At other times they carry electronic appliances or similar goods, but the paths of this exchange involves smuggling and personal relationships and is hard to trace. Using the knowledge of how stamp collecting works, there is some information to indicate how this trade functions. Stamps or even specially prepared envelopes are transported by Jewish couriers from Russia to Germany and Finland for further sale to collectors in the United States. This network utilizes relatives and even second- or third-cousins. Since at the moment the mail systems of much of the former Soviet Union is unreliable or nonexistent, such a network is very useful. How much other material travels this way is impossible to determine, but refugee populations of any nationality have always created such underground pathways. In an interview published with Mr. Satanowsky, one of the more successful Jewish businessmen in Russia, he stated: "We Russian Jewish businessmen can serve as a bridge between Western Jewish businessmen and managers in Russia."[14] Just how this would operate was not explained.

It is clear that the Russian area represents, once again, an eastern reservoir of Jews to reinforce the Jewish population of Germany. At the moment the best estimate seems to be that about one-third of the Jews in Germany are of Russian origin.

There is a group of Jews of Polish origin of considerable size in Germany, some of them in leadership positions. However, the destruction of the Polish Jewish community seems too complete to allow for a rebuilding of bridges. By all accounts there is still enough anti-Semitism in Poland to make an interchange between Jews and Poles almost impossible.

Contacts between the Jews of Germany and the Jews in Austria and the Danube basin are not close. The children of these groups may meet each other in summer camps, but neither Germany nor Austria has much to offer each other. The same is true of Swiss Jews, though there are a few printed magazines that go back and forth. Some Croatian and Bosnian Jews have fled to Germany, but their number is quite small.

The British Jewish community seems to have little contact with Germany today, although during World War II there was a considerable settlement of German Jews in England. The exception is the *Lubavitcher Chabad* in London, which serves as a center for all of Europe.

The new asylum regulations of Germany are designed to regulate and choke off the flow of new immigrants, including Jews. Anyone passing through a "safe" country such as Austria, the Czech Republic, or Poland will not be admitted. This will allow only wealthy Jews who can fly direct to Frankfurt from their own country to ask for asylum. Unless the German border guards are willing to shoot to kill illegal border-crossers, this new set of regulations will only slow the flow of "legal" asylum seekers, not of those determined to come to Germany at all costs.

Whether there will be a large inflow of Israelis into Germany will depend on the course of economic and political developments in Germany and Israel.

Until we can learn the birthrate of the Jews in Germany, as well as the composition of the inflow of Jews, it is impossible to estimate the composition of the Jewish community in Germany in the future nor to estimate what kind of international connections will develop when the Holocaust generation dies out.

NOTES

1. Toby Blum-Dobkin, *The Landsberg Carnival* in "Purim: The Face and the Mask" (New York: Yeshiva University Museum, 1979).

2. Personal observation.

3. Wolfgang Jacobmeyer, *Die Lager der Jüdischen Displaced Persons in den Deutschen West Zonen 1946–1947 als Orte der Jüdischen Selbstvegewisserung* in "Jüdisches Leben in Deutschland Seit 1945." 1988.

4. Ibid.

5. General Lucius D. Clay, *Decision in Germany*, p. 235. (New York: Doubleday, 1950).

6. Y. Michael Bodemann, *Staat und Ethnizitat: Der Aufbau der Jüdischen Gemeinden im Kalten Krieg* in "Jüdisches Leben in Deutschland seit 1945." 1988.

7. *Treaty of Luxemburg.*

8. H. G. Selethin, *Geschichte der Jüden in Berlin: Eine Festschrift der Jüdischen Gemeinde in Berlin*, 1959.

9. Y. Michael Bodemann, p. 68.

10. *Spiegel*, vol. 50, p. 92.

11. Lothar Mertens, *Alija: Die Emigration der Jüden aus der USSR/GUS* 2d ed. (Bochum: Universitatsverlag Dr. N. Brockmeyer, 1993), pp. 213–24.

12. Michael Wolffsohn, *Ewige Schuld? 40 Jahre Deutsch-Judisch-Israelische Beziehung* (Munich: Piper Actuell, 1988).

13. A. M. Rosenthal in *New York Times*, 24 Nov. 1992.

14. Walter Ruby, *Making It Big in the New Russia* in "Jewish World," 12 Feb. 1993.

Chapter Eight

In a Clouded Crystal Ball

Predicting the future is a dangerous occupation. Inaccurate visions of the future, as the Prophet Jonah found out at Nineveh, leave one sitting at the roadside, outside the gates, exposed to scorn. Prophets whose visions of the future turn out to be accurate do not have a much easier existence. Yet it is necessary to point out trends that will influence the future of the Jews of Germany.

The official Jewish community and the nonmembers of the *Gemeinde* who admit their Jewish heritage seem to be solidly established as a permanent Jewish presence in the German Republic, always barring a political catastrophe. The number of congregations is increasing rapidly in both the former East and West Germany, as is the number of young people who participate in Jewish affairs. Despite the present economic depression, job opportunities continue to exist for immigrants, not only for those who come from Russia, but also those who come to Germany from developed nations and from Israel. Exact figures of Jewish economic life are hard to determine, but a general sense of economic well-being can be felt in the Jewish community.[1] Most of the older immigrants are being supported by the German social network, while the younger Jews can be found working in business, the sciences, medicine, the arts, and other white-collar jobs. There seems to be no discrimination against Jews in the job market, and some of the larger firms seem anxious to hire Jews so as to prove their cultural diversity and freedom from Nazi taint.

What seems to be totally missing among the Jews of Germany today is a working class. Many Russians, especially those from the big cities like St. Petersburg, Moscow, and Kiev, are trained in academic pursuits. The younger ones may not find jobs yet at the level to which their training would entitle them, but they usually do find employment in their professional fields. Among the German, Israeli, and Polish Jews, there are entrepreneurs, artists, writers, scientists, and storekeepers but few or no craftsmen or industrial workers. This job distribution givers the next generation of Jews a better chance to find employment in computer fields, medicine, or finance, but it increases their frustration if their job hunt has inadequate success. Such seeming "failure" has social as well as economic consequences in the Jewish community. Income and social acceptance are often connected. Some of these unsuccessful job-seekers will probably either emigrate or turn radical.

Among the Jews of Germany the old spirit of venture entrepreneurship flourishes. Like the economic life of the old ghettos, very little of this activity flows through the big banks or stock exchanges. Financing is done by a private network of associates. Jewish banks such as Warburg in Hamburg or Rothschild in Frankfurt are as little used by these entrepreneurs as are the purely German financial houses. Many of the financially successful Jews began their economic rise by opening small, commercial enterprises in West Germany. They ran food stores, clothing stores, or night clubs. From there they went on, in some cases, to the jewelry trade. Quite a few of such fine jewelers can be found today in both Frankfurt and Berlin. Their connections to the Jewish gem dealers in Tel Aviv, Amsterdam, and New York helped them when they began building their businesses in the late 1950s and early 1960s. Surplus funds generated by the jewelry or other business was invested in German real estate. However, these merchants did not give up their old fields; they simply added real-estate management to their other activities. Some of them also acquired property by purchasing reparations claims from emigrés overseas who preferred to let others maneuver their claims through the intricate German bureaucracy. The usual method was for the buyer to advance a small sum and then pay a much larger amount if the claim was successful. Many claims for property in Berlin and East Germany are still pending, and a small army of lawyers and government officials are working hard to clear the clogged dockets. The meteoric rise in the value of German real estate after the unification of Germany has made some of these operators very rich individuals. Unlike some of the Jewish tycoons in the United States and Britain, these self-made Jewish millionaires, or even billionaires, avoid the limelight and conspicuous consumption. They want to avoid the unfavorable publicity that was used by the anti-Semites of the 1920s to smear the Jews in general.

Additional funds from Jewish-owned firms in the United States have also been invested recently in German urban real estate. With the money came a group of Americans who act as investment counselors, lawyers, and administrators. The Jewish members of this group join the *Gemeinde*, thus adding another nationality to the Jewish mixture in Germany.

There is an increasing Jewish visibility in Germany. The Jews are no longer being pictured only as aging victims of the Holocaust; they are seen also as bearers of a viable culture and as participants in the total life of Germany. Some Jews have become active in German cultural and charitable affairs as well as continuing their roles in the Jewish community. This, of course, does not make Jews into Germans, but it does make them part of the German scene today.

In Berlin, increasingly the focal point of Germany, non-Jews as well as Jews visit the Jewish museum, attend workshops on Jewish culture at the Centrum Judaicum and the Jewish high school and eat at the Jewish restaurants around the old Jewish district. One of them, *Oron*, specializes in Israeli food and is already so popular that it is difficult to get a seat there at lunchtime. Learning about Jewish culture has become "trendy" in some German circles, and young Germans can sometimes be found visiting religious ceremonies in the synagogues out of curiosity. The gilding on the dome and the neo-Moorish facade of the "New Synagogue" can be taken as a symbol of the new Jewish assertiveness and visibility.

There is no question that there is and will continue to be anti-Semitism in Germany. Some of this takes the form of hoodlums vandalizing a Jewish cemetery, a Holocaust memorial, or even beating up an individual who "looks Jewish." More insidious is the now-acceptable conversation in some circles about "Jewish money" and "Jewish political influence." Steffan Heitmann, the former candidate for German president of the CDU, has made such conversation more respectable by his public comment that Germany cannot be judged forever by the Nazi era. This kind of "salon anti-Semitism" can be expected to become more common as reparations continue to be paid out by a government faced with budget deficits. It can also be expected to increase as investments by Jewish-owned firms become more visible. It will certainly increase if any irregularities are uncovered in the awarding of contracts for the construction of office buildings to any Jewish-owned real-estate firm. Jews will be condemned as "Jewish blood suckers" if they participate in German development, and they will be condemned if they are poor as an "unjustified drain by foreigners on the German social system" among some people. Since these conversations, rumors, and innuendos do not constitute overt actions, they are very difficult to combat. The more open enemies of the Jewish communities can also be expected to increase with the continuation of unemployment and social pressures in Germany. It can be anticipated that the Republican Party, the most antiforeign and nationalistic of the legal German political parties, will cross the 5-percent threshold and will be able to elect a representative or two to sit in the *Bundestag*, the national parliament, and they will use that status to move from being a fringe group to some respectability. The Republicans have already elected representatives to a number of local legislative bodies.

However, the "anti-foreign," that is, the anti-Jewish, platform of some Germans is diffused by the existence of a multiplicity of targets of xenophobia. Turks, homosexuals, Sinti and Roma, Arabs, and Africans all offer targets for those who wish to hate all that is not "pure German."

The federal German government, both at present and in the foreseeable future, intends to take strong action against any overt expression of these hatreds, as far as the German law permits. This is true particularly in the upper echelons of government, not necessarily among the local police or the local judges. This federal activity is partly in self-defense. The memories of the cost of a Hitler or the street fighting between radical political gangs of the Right and Left that preceded the rise of the Third Reich go far beyond any moral considerations. Nor is this fear of the past confined to the government. Many of the average citizens express an unwillingness to vote for any radical party, even if they agree intellectually with that party's program. The fear of a repetition of the past is stronger than any wish for radical reform. This is true of the younger as well as the older Germans, especially in the urban centers. The extremist groups are aware of this factor of fear and exploit it by using violence in their demonstrations. Most Germans will avoid such violent confrontations at almost any cost, a characteristic of German culture that might help explain the rise of the Nazis and the noninterference of most Germans with the Nazi excesses, even when such interference was still possible.

The daily life of the Jews in Germany must deal with the present and with the strengthening of Jewish culture rather than engage in lamentations on the Holocaust. As a spokesman for the Jewish community in Berlin told us: "The building of a Holocaust memorial, a *Mahnmal*, is a function and responsibility of the German state. The building of a Jewish museum and the choosing of a director for it should be our concern."[2] A specific "Day of Remembrance," as it is celebrated in the United States and Israel, is not on the Jewish religious calendar in Germany, though many memorials dealing with the Holocaust are marked.[3]

This does not mean that the Holocaust is pushed into the background or that the damage it has done to European Jewry can be repaired. Any present revival of Nazism stirs up the old wounds and forces the Jewish leaders to speak out. They always hope to be joined in their protests by others, but if necessary they speak out alone. The "missing" six million Jews have not been replaced. The Jews in Germany are increasing in numbers by transfers from other Jewish communities, not by a massive increase of the birthrate or by conversions. The Orthodox Jews will probably continue to have many children; the less Orthodox, somewhat fewer births. This birthrate will simply maintain the size of the Jewish community, not rebuild it to its former numbers. Marriages between Jews and non-Jews are fairly common in Germany as elsewhere, and it is unknown still how many of their offspring will number themselves among the Jews.

Nor can the loss of the Yiddish-speaking cultures of the *stedl* be made good. Yiddish is not on the curriculum of the newly established Jewish high school in Berlin. Exhibits of photographs and artifacts of the old Jewish life are similar to the exhibits of the ethnography of any extinct tribal culture. They do not turn what is now a dead past into a living, vibrant heritage. As an older singer of Jewish folk songs admitted to us: "My Yiddish is becoming more and more tinged with German pronunciation."[4] Many performers of the traditional Jewish *klezmer* music of the ghettos today are non-Jews. The old Yiddish songs have become part of the repertoire of folk singers as are the Scottish ballads and American cowboy songs.

Israeli songs and Israeli-style celebrations of the holidays may serve as a replacement for the loss of the Yiddish culture. Dances and songs of Israeli origin are greeted by Jewish audiences in Germany with an enthusiasm not given to the old Yiddish music.

Many of the Jews in Germany have visited Israel and have relatives there so the Israeli styles are familiar. Israeli crafts and Israeli foods are found in stores in Germany. Some of the local Jewish papers carry advertisements asking for contributions for institutions in Israel. Zionist organizations are active in Germany, but their support for the actual settlement of Jews in Germany in Israel is more vocal than realistic.

The community of Jews in Germany is also facing some massive, internal changes. One of these is determined by the fact that the Holocaust generation is disappearing. New leadership with new outlooks is coming to the forefront, although many of the important positions in the communities are still held by old-timers. This also means that the old ad hoc organization of the Jewish communities, which grew according to need, will have to be put on a more formal basis. How are the votes on the *Zentralrat* to be allocated? At the moment some of the seats are allocated to city organizations with thousands of members, such as Frankfurt, Munich, or Berlin. Other seats represent regional organizations such as Thuringia with a mere 250 members or even smaller local organizations. Who judges the standards of the new synagogues both in terms of finances and ritual before they are admitted to the general body of German *Gemeinden*? What methods will different communities use to adjudicate claims to various geographic territories and pieces of property of the old congregations? In many cases no formal rules seem to exist, but the problem of drawing up a new constitution to govern the *Gemeinden* of Germany is being studied by committees set up by the *Zentralrat*.

A new method of generating additional funds for social and welfare services will have to be set up since the assets generated by sale of returned surplus property no longer needed by the *Gemeinden* are used up. So far, local or state governments have made up the deficits of the individual *Gemeinden*, but it is by no means certain whether this system will continue in the future political and economic climate. As in the United States, voluntary contributions are being solicited from individuals to fill gaps in the government-supported programs. Such a system gives a stronger voice to the wealthier members of the congregations, despite the theoretical equality of all voting members. These are technical and organizational problems that can be dealt with by rational discussion. The other problems that are appearing along with the new generation are more difficult to solve, since they involve philosophy and social outlook, subjects that are not decided solely by rational thought.

There are increasing strains on the concept of the united communities, the *Einheitsgemeinde*. On the "Liberal" side there is discussion of the role of women in modern society that no longer lets a number of women be satisfied with being seated in the balcony of the synagogue and relegated to the auxiliary organizations of the community. They want to do more than light the Sabbath candles and recite the blessings while the men discuss both finances and the *Talmud*. Waiting uneasily in the wings are the questions of ordination of female rabbis, the role of single parents in the Jewish community, and the thorny problem of homosexuality. Sooner or later, the Jews of Germany must make decisions on these questions as the Jewish community moves past the question of mere survival.

Among the Orthodox there is increasing emphasis on fulfilling all parts of the traditional Jewish law. This entails the construction of ritual baths, obtaining adequate amounts of carefully supervised kosher foods, and increasing the limitations on permissible activities on the Sabbath. It also means that facilities must be found for worshippers who must travel to a synagogue and stay overnight since travel is prohibited on Friday night. It also causes further restrictions on contacts between Orthodox Jews and others, both Jews and members of other religions. Sooner or later the Orthodox must also find a system to bring in rabbis adequately trained to handle the many problems of Jewish law. This is a function that has so far remained by default of availability of local authorities to Israeli and American scholars. Even with telephones and fax machines, such a process is clumsy. Here, the role of the *Lubavitcher*

Hasidim needs to be determined, since *Hasidism* is only one form of Orthodox Judaism.

For both Orthodox and Liberals, it is found that Jewish museums and exhibitions are only of peripheral value in holding the Jewish community together, no matter how useful these exhibits are in showing Jewish objects and photographs to non-Jews. Unlike medieval Christianity when cathedrals and rituals held the community together, Judaism is a religion of philosophy and debate. No number of beautiful candelabra or the construction of fine synagogue buildings can replace the verbal interaction among the different parts of the community. The younger generation will need much training in Jewish discussion before the old patterns of Judaism can be restored or new patterns developed.

The reorganization of the Jewish community, both as a central organization for all of Germany and a presence in more cities, will force individual Jews to make personal decisions as well. Individuals and families, especially those with children, will have to decide whether to identify themselves as Jews and, if so, what kind of Jews. As the Jewish presence in Germany has grown, so have the number of choices available.

Some individuals will opt to become "silent Jews." These are Jews who are fully aware that they are Jews or have Jewish ancestry. They often prefer to give no outward sign of their belonging to this minority. They are not members of the *Gemeinde* nor do they practice any of the rituals of Judaism. They often honor the Jewishness of one or both of their parents. They are aware that in some circles they might be considered "not quite German," but they simply avoid situations or groups where their ethnic or religious affiliation—or lack—becomes a problem. They do not usually convert to another religion; they remain unaffiliated.

A number of other individuals will choose the path of Liberal Judaism. They join the *Gemeinde* and attend some of its functions or those of some alternative Jewish group. Their social circle is likely to be primarily Jewish and even some of their business associates will be "of their own kind." This definition of their "own kind" might lead to a further subdivision into German Jews, Polish Jews, or Russian-speaking Jews. As mentioned in earlier chapters, these ethnic divisions still play a considerable role in Jewish life in Germany. Such differentiation is only possible in the larger congregations or communities where enough Jews exist to divide themselves into groups.

A relatively small number will choose the path of Orthodoxy. This means deliberate separation from the Germans in home life and in the business world. So far the outward signs of Orthodoxy, the traditional black suits and head coverings, are not seen on the streets of Germany but are reserved for religious occasions. The few who do dress that way are usually outsiders, *Hasids* from other countries or Orthodox from Israel or the United States. This custom might change, as it has in the United States, and the dress of eighteenth-century Poland will reappear on the streets of the old Jewish *Scheunenviertel*.

The *Lubavitchers*, though few in number, play a crucial role. They consider themselves missionaries rather than pulpit rabbis of congregations.[5] They feel their mission is to spread "Jewishness" among all Jews, not to live isolated among the like-minded Orthodox. Because they are so visible, wearing Orthodox dress and giving public interviews about themselves and their mission, they are often consulted to define the Orthodox Jewish position even among those who are not Orthodox themselves. This will continue until Germany once more has its own Yeshiva or a sufficient number of Orthodox rabbis imported from Israel or the United States,

A trip to Israel or sending the children to school or summer camp there is very common among the Jews in Germany. Since many non-Jewish Germans also visit Israel, such a visit is not an outward sign of Judaism. A trip to Israel can be but does not have to be a personal pilgrimage and need have nothing to do with official Judaism or religious affiliation. Many of the half-Jews, for instance, have taken one or more such trips.

None of these avenues will avoid the psychological problem of dual identity. Most of the Jews in Germany are aware of the disapproval of the Jews of other countries that they chose to live in Germany. One of a visiting delegation of United Jewish Agency (UJA) officials from the United States expressed it recently: "Should Germany make itself so attractive to Jews fleeing the former Soviet Union when Israel so badly wants these immigrants? And should American Jews view the commitment, energy and flavor of Berlin's small Jewish community with sadness, joy or a mixture of the two?" These questions came after deploring the ambivalent stand of Germany toward foreigners.[6] The fact that American Jews feel free to make such judgments even today shows the strength of preconceptions abroad, as do the comments of "small Jewish community in Berlin" for a community with an official membership of 10,000. The Israelis, of course, are still ambivalent about the fact that there are any Jews in Germany.

This international attitude and the varieties of Judaism available do nothing to avoid the fact that the Jews are aware they are considered non-Germans by most of the German population. Even conversion to Christianity or atheism does not solve this problem of ambiguity of identity, nor does belonging to the most Orthodox of the branches of Judaism help. This confusion of identity is characteristic of all minorities in all countries of the world. It will not disappear in the foreseeable future in Germany, even if all the Jews were given immediate German citizenship.

There are political splits as well among the Jewish groups in Germany, splits that are becoming more public as the size and visibility of the Jews in Germany increase. Some Jews are now taking a more active role in support of the Christian Democrats and the Free Democrats, roles that tend to balance the overt presence of Jews in the parties of the Left. The recent public attacks by Ignatz Bubis on the candidacy of Steffan Heitmann of the CDU focussed attention on such Jewish conservative politicians since Bubis is an avowed member of the Free Democrats. Bubis attacked Heitmann's candidacy both as an individual and as head of the *Zentralrat*, thus sharing the position of the left-wingers but also showing that they are not the only Jewish anti-Nazis. There is already disagreement within the Jewish community about the question of the actions of the Israeli government regarding the Palestinians and other Arabs. Further disagreements, some of them quite strident, can be expected to occur. There is no disagreement on the opposition to any form of right-wing extremism, no matter against whom that extremism is directed. There all Jews are united. These splits within the Jewish community can be considered a sign of strength, since they are only possible in a community that does not feel the necessity to show closed ranks on any and all occasions.

The problem of mixed marriages shows no sign of abating. At a recent youth congress in Frankfurt sponsored by the *Zentralrat*, over two hundred participants discussed the issue by drawing on their personal experiences.[7] These were not only the children of such marriages; they are people who are members of such unions today and now face the problem of deciding to what group their children belong. For those who wish to affiliate with Judaism, the religion of the mother should be decisive, but the world at large reckons descent by the father. The parents in each case must now decide if they wish to belong to one group or the other or if they can belong to no group at all. In a country like the United States, this problem is not too serious, but in the daily life in Germany religious identification, even if not formal membership in a religious body, is often a public matter, particularly in the smaller towns.

The curriculum and publicity about the new Jewish high school in Berlin that opened in August 1993 may show the parameters of the future of the Jews in Germany. There is compulsory instruction in Hebrew and in Jewish culture. The food that is served to the students for the midday meal is kosher, and a prayer is said by the entire student body daily. There are both Christian students and Christian teachers in the school, but all staff members have been trained in Israel. Jerzy Kanal, chairman of the Jewish community in Berlin, emphasized to the press that he considered the opening of the school another step in the reestablishment of Jewish culture in Berlin. There was the customary reference to the Holocaust and its survivors, but the emphasis was on the present and the future, not on the past.[8]

NOTES

1. Personal observation.

2. Interview with Ted Ambros, August 1993.

3. Interview with Jerzy Kanal, chairman of the Berlin Jewish community, August 1993.

4. Interview in the *Kulturverein*, Summer 1993.

5. *Interview with Rav Israel Diskin* in "Jewish Week," Munich 1993.

6. Toby Axelrod, *A Tale of Two Cities* in "The Jewish Week," 11 Nov. 1993.

7. *Jewish Week*, Munich 1993.

8. Interviews published in all Berlin newspapers, 6 Aug. 1993.

Glossary

Allgemeine Jüdische Wochenzeitung—(General Jewish Weekly Newspaper) issued in Bonn for the entire Jewish community in Germany. Abbreviated as *"Allgemeine."*

Ashkenazi—Jewish traditions and ritual derived from the customs of German and Austrian Jews. Also applied to all Jews from Europe who follow these traditions.

Austrittsgesetz—(Law of Separation) passed the German legislature in 1894 to allow individuals to leave the *Gemeinde* without losing their status as Jews or allowing congregations to separate themselves from the main body of the community.

Blau-Weiss—(Blue-White) German Zionist organization specializing in outdoor activity 1919–1929.

Bundesrepublik—(BDR) Federal republic organized in 1948 covering the British, American, and French zones of occupation in West Germany.

Bundestag—Lower house of the German legislature.

Christian Democratic Union—(CDU) The more conservative of the two major parties of Germany with ties to the Catholic hierarchy. Especially strong in the Rhineland and Bavaria.

Concentration Camp—(KZ) Originally internment camps for political prisoners, they later became, in many cases, extermination camps.

Displaced Persons—(DP) Term used by occupying powers for all non-German refugees in Germany 1945–1950.

Eastern Jews—Term used to describe all Jews originating in what today are Belarus, Estonia, Croatia, Hungary, Latvia, Lithuania, Moldova, Poland, Roumania, Russia, and the Ukraine.

Einheitsgemeinde—(Unity Community) A Jewish community that includes Jews following Liberal, Conservative, and Orthodox rituals.

Einsatzkommando—(Special Mission Task Force) German military units used for the extermination of all Jews in ghettos by shooting. Often composed of Lithuanians and Ukrainians as well as Austrians and Germans.

Frankfurt on the Main—Town in Western Germany noted for banking and its large community of Jews. To be distinguished from Frankfurt on the Oder in Eastern Germany.

Free Democrats—Party often forming the junior partner in the ruling government of Germany. Strongly business oriented.

Gemeinde—(Community) Jewish community that may include one or more synagogues, social services, and schools as well as other facilities run by a *Gemeinderat* or community board elected by its members.

German Democratic Republic—(DDR) East German government established in 1948 in the Russian zone of occupation. The government of the DDR followed the Soviet line in economic, social, and foreign affairs. The DDR collapsed in 1989 and was absorbed in the united Germany in 1990.

Gestapo—(*Geheime Staats-Polizei*) Nazi secret police.

Ghetto—The Jewish settlement or part of town, formerly surrounded by walls. Reestablished in Poland by the Nazis.

Gulag—Russian concentration camp.

Halacha—Jewish ritual law.

Hasidim—Jewish sect originating in Poland in the eighteenth century and emphasizing a more personal interaction with religion than can be obtained by merely studying the *Torah* or *Talmud*. *Hasidic* services often include dancing and singing outdoors.

Judenfrei—(Free of Jews) Applied by Nazis to streets or towns where Jews were prohibited. This policy eventually led to the "Final Solution," the attempt to exterminate all Jews in Europe.

Judenrat—(Jewish Council) appointed by the Nazis to carry out the administration and Nazi policies in a ghetto.

Kibbutz—Jewish communal settlement in Israel.

Kosher—(Clean) Ritually permissible food or clothing.

Kristallnacht—(Night of Broken Glass) November 9–10, 1938, when all Jewish stores and institutions were vandalized and set ablaze. Many Jews were arrested that night and about 100 were killed.

Kulturverein—(Jewish Cultural Club) Jewish organization stressing Jewish cultural rather than ritual tradition.

Landjuden—(Country Jews) Jews living in the small towns and villages in Germany for centuries. They were usually Orthodox in ritual orientation.

Lingua Franca—Hybrid language used for communication between groups of differing nationality.

Lubavitcher—*Hasidic* group originating in the town of *Lubavitch* in Poland and now headquartered in Brooklyn, New York.

Maccabi—Jewish athletic association named after the leaders of the Jewish revolt against Syria 167 B.C.

Nazis—(National Socialist Workers Party of Germany) Hitler's political party. The term is used interchangeably for the members of the party and the German government 1933–1945.

Rabbi—Originally used as an honorific for any Jew skilled in Jewish law. Now usually designates someone who has graduated from a Jewish religious school and has been ordained.

Republican Party—Most right-wing of the legal German political parties, strongly antiforeign.

Sabbath—Holy day of rest that runs from sundown Friday to sundown Saturday. No work or travel is to be undertaken on this day, according to Jewish ritual law.

Schaliach—Emissaries or missionaries. The term is usually applied to *Lubavitcher Hasidim* who serve in that role.

Scheunenviertel—(Hay barn district) Old Jewish district in Berlin.

Sephardim—Jewish customs and traditions originating in Spain before the expulsion of the Jews in 1492. Now applied to all Oriental Jews and their customs.

Silesia—District east of the Oder River that has been often disputed between Poland and Prussia. It is now Poland, with its capital in Poznans (Posen).

Stedl—(Small City or Town) Usually applied to the small towns in Poland and Russia with large Jewish populations.

Synagogue—Jewish house of assembly for worship and study. The term "Temple" is usually reserved for the Temple in Jerusalem destroyed by the Romans in A.D. 72.

Talmud—The traditional Jewish law and learning written down after the destruction of the Temple and extensively commented on since.

Third Reich—Hitler's Germany. The second Reich was the German Empire 1871–1918. The first Reich was the Holy Roman Empire of the German Nation, 800–1812 A.D.

Torah—The first five books of the Bible, written on scrolls by hand and displayed on holy days in the synagogue.

Yeshiva—Jewish school for advanced learning.

Yiddish—Jewish language or dialect based on medieval German with many Hebrew and local loan words. It is usually written in Hebrew letters.

Zentralrat—(Central Council) Governing body for all Jewish communities in Germany.

Selected Bibliography

BOOKS

Aleichem, Sholom. *Tevye's Daughters*. Translated by Frances Butwin. 2 vols. New York: Crown Publishers, 1949.

Amsberg, Peter. *Geschichte der Frankfurter Juden*. Darmstadt: Raether Verlag, 1983.

Baumann, Zygmunt. *Modernity and the Holocaust*. Ithaca, N.Y.: Cornell University Press, 1989.

Bilderarchiv Preussichen Kulturbesitz. Juden in Preussen. Dortmund: Harenberg Kommunikation, 1981.

Brumlick, Micha, ed. *Jüdisches Leben in Deutschland Seit 1945*. Frankfurt: Jüdischer Verlag bei Atheneum, 1988.

Bubis, Ignatz (with Edith Kohn). *Ich bin ein Deutscher Staatsbürger Jüdischen Glaubens*. Köln: Kiepenhauer & Witsch, 1993.

Bundesgesetzblatt 1953 No. 5 Pt. 2. *Agreement Between the Bundesrepublic Germany and the State of Israel*, Signed September 10, 1952.

Burgauer, Erica. *Zwischen Erinnerung und Verdrängung-Juden in Deutschland Nach 1945*. Hamburg: Rowolt, 1993.

Clay, General Lucius D. *Decision in Germany*. Garden City, N.Y.: Doubleday & Co., 1950.

Cohn, Michael, ed. *From Germany to Washington Heights*. New York: Yeshiva University Museum, 1987.

Dundas, Alan. *Cracking Jokes*. Berkeley, CA.: 10 Speed Press, 1987.

Gay, Peter. *The Berlin Jewish Spirit*. Leo Baeck Memorial Lecture No. 15: New York, 1972.

Geisel, Eike, ed. *Im Scheunenviertel*. Berlin: Severin and Seidel, 1981.

Gilbert, Martin. *A Jewish Historical Atlas*. New York: William Morrow, 1993.

Heimreich, William B. *Against All Odds*. New York: Simon and Schuster, 1992.

Hertzberg, Arthur. *The Zionist Idea*. New York: Atheneum, 1969.

Hirschler, Gertrude, ed. *Ashkenaz, The German Jewish Heritage*. New York: Yeshiva University Museum, 1987.

Lefkowitz, Deborah. *Interval of Silence: Being Jewish in Germany*. Cambridge, MA.: Lefkowitz Films, 1990.

Lowe, Adolph. *In Memoriam: Franz Oppenheimer* in "Leo Baeck Yearbook," 1965.

Luel, Steven A., and Marcus, Paul, ed. *Psychoanalytical Reflections on the Holocaust*. New York: KTAV Publishing House, 1984.

Mead, Margaret. *Israel and the Problem of Identity*. New York: Herzl Institute, 1958.

Mertens, Lothar. *Alija: Die Emigration der Juden aus der USSR/GUS*, 2d ed. Bochum: Universitätsverlag, Dr. N. Brockmeyer. 1993.

Nachama, Andreas, and Schoeps, Julius H. *Aufbau Nach Dem Untergang*. Berlin: Argon, 1992.

Offenberg, Mario. *Adass Jisroel: Vernichted und Vergessen*. Berlin, DDR: Museumspädagogischer Dienst, 1986.

Opiz, Georg Emanuel. *Ein Zeichner der Leipziger Messe*. Leipziger Messeamt, 1986.

Ostow, Robin. *Jüdisches Leben in der DDR*. Frankfurt: Jüdischer Verlag bei Atheneum, 1988.

Postal, Bernard, and Abramson, Samuel A. *Landmarks of a People*. New York: Hill & Wang, 1962.

Rosmus, Anna. *Wintergrün-Verdrängte Morde*. Konstanz: Labhard Publishers, 1993.

Runge, Irene. *Von Kommen und Bleiben*. Auslandbeauftragte des Senats von Berlin, 1992.

Rurup, Reinhard. *Topographie des Terrors*. Berlin: Verlag Willmuth Arenhovel, 1987.

Saigh, P. A., ed. *Post Traumatic Stress Disorder*. New York: Pergamon Press, 1992.

Seeliger, Herbert. *Origin and Growth of the Berlin Jewish Community* in "Leo Baeck Yearbook," 1958.

Seidel, Peter. *Germany for the Jewish Traveller*. Bonn: German Tourist Office, 1991.

Selethin, H. G. *Geschichte der Jüden in Berlin*. Festschrift der Jüdischen Gemeinde Berlin, 1959.

Shirer, William L. *The Rise and Fall of the Third Reich*. New York: Simon & Schuster, 1960.

Sichlrovsky, Peter, ed. *Strangers in Their Own Land*. New York: Basic Books, 1986.

Sigal, John J., and Weinfeld, Morton. *Trauma and Rebirth: Intergenerational Effect of the Holocaust*. Westport, CT.: Praeger, 1989.

Silbernagl, Isador. *Verfassung und Verwaltung Sämtlicher Religionsgemeinschaften in Bayern*, 4th ed. Regensburg: 1900.

Stern, Susan and Neuger, James G. *Ten Went West*. Atlantik: Brücke, 1993.

Weyden, Peter. *Stella*. New York: Simon & Schuster, 1992.

U.S. Dept. of State. *Occupation of Germany: Policy and Progress 1945–1946*. Publication 2783, Washington, DC: Government Printing Office, 1947.

Wigoder, Geoffrey, ed. *Encyclopedia Judaica*. 4 vols. New York: Macmillan, 1972.

Wild, Dieter, ed. *Juden und Deutsche*. Hamburg: *Spiegel* Special No. 2, 1992.

Willett, John. *Art and Politics in the Weimar Period*. New York: Pantheon Books, 1978.

Wolffsohn, Michael. *Eternal Guilt? Forty Years of German-Jewish-Israeli Relations*. Translated by Douglas Bokovoy. New York: Columbia University Press, 1993.

Yahil, Leni. *The Holocaust: The Fate of European Jewry 1941–45*. Oxford University Press, 1990.

PERIODICALS

Allgemeine Jüdische Wochenzeitung, Bonn

Berliner Umschau, Berlin Gemeinde

Bund Bulletin. World Coordinating Committee of Bundists and Affiliated Jewish Socialist Organizations, New York

Hamburger Abendblatt, Hamburg
International Herald Tribune, Paris
Jewish Chronicle, London
Jewish Week, New York
Jewish World, New York
Jüdische Korrespondenz, Berlin, *Jüdischer Kulturverein*
Nachrichtenblatt des Verbandes der Jüdischen Gemeinden der DDR,
    Berlin 1987–1988
New York Times
Semittimes: Das Deutsch-Judisches Meinungs und Zeitmagazin.
Der Spiegel, Hamburg
Unabhangische Jüdische Stimme, Berlin

Index

About the Author

MICHAEL COHN is Adjunct Anthropologist at the Yeshiva University Museum in New York City. He has served at the Brooklyn Children's Museum for 25 years and is the author of many works on minorities and history, particularly of the New York area.

ISBN 0-275-94878-1

EAN

9 780275 948788

90000>